WE NEED TO TALK ABOUT THE CONDITIONS OF MY IMPRISONMENT
...and other parenting stories

An Anthology of Quirky and Unusual
Parenting Tales
Compiled by

Michelle Tan

<u>WE NEED TO TALK ABOUT THE CONDITIONS OF MY</u>
<u>IMPRISONMENT</u>

First Published 2018 by Wallace Publishing
www.wallacepublishing.co.uk

Cover art by Steve Williams
www.saa.co.uk/art/stevewilliamsart

Contents

Dedication 4

Foreword 5

A Fairy Tale for the Perfect Mother 8

The Toddler Highway Code 14

Eating Out, Toddler Style 17

Pre-Schooler CV 21

Checklist: Is Your Child Gifted? 25

The Green Food Strike 31

Where Do Babies Come From? 34

Why Can't We Have Sex Like the Coneheads? 38

Together Against PENIS 41

Advice for New Parents 45

Just Call Me Secret Mum… 49

Eight Women You Need to Avoid… 52

The Egg Wars 57

Beauty and the Beast (A Parody) 62

Mummy Princess Goes to a Meeting 71

The Play Date 75

10 Rules of Hotel Etiquette 80

Dear Neighbours in Our Apartment Complex 84

Peppa Pig More Addictive Than Cocaine… 88

School Run Section Added to Driving Theory Test ... 93

We Need to Talk About the Conditions… 96

Dedication

Dedicated to our children:

Kyle, Claire and Jay
Eli and Zachariah
Ivy Rhisa and Freddie
Buddy and Edith
Matilda and Amelia
Joshua
Harry and Oliver
Jared
Ernest and Olive
Luke, Zak and Ben
Holly Isobel and Abigail Rose
Kyran and Ava
Isobel and Thomas
Carly, Addison, Hazel and Elizabeth
Jackson and Cooper
Killian, Dominic, Bob and Clara
Aidan and Nathaniel
Ben, Frankie and Alice
Siena, Saffron and Jack
Jet and Stella
Grace and Elise

Foreword

By Harriet Shearsmith

Modern parenting is a bit like running a televised marathon in a ball gown with poo being flung at you from all directions at times, isn't it? We're constantly on display. Constantly trying to navigate the sleepless nights, poonamis, spit-ups and, worst of all, the judgement that comes flying in from left, right and centre whilst it feels like everyone else popped a baby out, went straight to Instagram with their totally profesh birthing photos and was awarded their Facebook "Fountain Of All Baby-based Knowledge" award within forty-two minutes of breastfeeding like a well-seasoned milking cow.

Everyone seems to have it more together than you do. Everyone else seems to have harnessed that glorious "natural" parental instinct that you left at the baby shop before the stork made its presence known. Everyone else managed to birth with only gas and air, don't you know? They're also breastfeeding without any pain and they are totally rocking this motherhood malarkey... and then there is you.

Well, you came to the right place. I was so honoured when I was asked to write this foreword for Lucy and Michelle because for once, I felt like there wasn't going to be any side-eye for admitting that my children went to school with a Belvita in hand and yesterday's jumper on because it was the first week back at school and we had all slept in. There wasn't going to be the awkward silence if I said that sometimes I sit on the kitchen floor by the door because it's the easiest place to make a quick escape and it's the furthest point in the house away from the children, so I can have five minutes away from their bickering. There was no shock when I said that motherhood is nothing like I envisioned it would be and that I'm not remotely the mother that the perky-breasted twenty-year-old me thought I would be. Not at all.

Modern parenting has become harder and harder because we're on display and everyone thinks they are an expert. So consider this book the antithesis to that. No one in his book is an expert, or would claim to be. These posts are written by real people, on the frontline of parenthood, where they have failed at one thing, and won at another. They have felt the sting of the judgemental "perfect" mum and they have been force-fed her image from the second they nearly shit themselves when that little blue line came up on the test. Every parent, no matter how perfect you might perceive them to be in comparison to you, has a story where their child was what can only be affectionately described as 'Satan spawn'. Every parent has had a moment when they've thought "I wonder if I can get a refund?" Every parent has had a giggle at themselves at the end of the day because they've stared at their kids sleeping long enough to be slightly creepy and thought, "Yeah, I'd do anything for you", only to follow that thought up with a gymnastic performance to exit the floor without stepping on the creaking floorboard.

These are those stories, those relatable moments that are far from perfect but make the bones and reality of parenthood. Enjoy!

ABOUT HARRIET SHEARSMITH

Harriet Shearsmith is a mother of three small (feral) children and the creator behind Toby&Roo, a parenting and lifestyle blog that aims to share the wins and woes of her family life and parenting journey (whatever that means). Harriet lives in the countryside of North Yorkshire, where absolutely nothing happens, with her husband, aforementioned children, two dogs, five cats, and two guinea pigs who are begrudgingly new additions to the family. Harriet's passions are writing, stalking her children for Instagrammable photos (no ugly ones, thanks. #delete), and cooking when the children aren't around to bring on the neurotic eye twitch that is an almost permanent feature. To relax, she would read and indulge in hot baths, but that's pure speculation as she can't really remember those days...

A Fairy Tale for the Perfect Mother

Once upon a time, in a home not far from yours, in a charming suburb called 'Bullshit', there lived a beautifully perfect Mother. The Mother had the most Perfect Child, the most perfectly cleaned and vacuumed home, and lived the most perfect life. What was most perfect of all in her perfectly decorated little home was a beautiful golden gilded Magical Mirror, which hung proudly in a walk-in wardrobe which was as big as your pathetic bedroom.

This morning, like every morning, right after doing her Sun Salutation yoga pose, the Perfect Mother, whom we will name Adina, looked at her Magical Mirror and smiled.

'Mirror, mirror, on the wall, who's the most Perfect Mother of all?' she asked.

Even the people moving in next door, the rumbling of the moving truck, the yelling, the screams of the children, did not wake her own child up.

The mirror fogged slightly, and said in a light lilt, 'You are, of course, lovely Adina, the most Perfect Mother of ALL!'

With a big self-congratulatory smile and a self-pat on her firm ass, Adina took her baby to the local coffee club to warmly welcome the rest of her Morning Coffee Group, a group she had calmly ruled as Her Royal Highness, Queen Mother of All Things Mothering since she had given birth. Adina queened it at morning coffee, as usual, with everyone bowing their heads in deference as she spoke of the food she would prepare, growing, grinding and pounding the ingredients from scratch; the clothes she would sew by hand;

and the baby poo that would be reused in her garden as fertilizer.

It was just another perfect day in the perfect life of the Perfect Mother. As she laid her head to sleep on her duck feather pillow, she dreamt of standing on a stage, in front of a podium, giving a lecture to a massive audience on the subject of 'how parents should not use their children as a convenient excuse to be lazy and dirty'. But, like all good fairy tales, something shitty was about to happen and change everything.

The next morning, the sun peeped through the window and awoke Adina so gently. She yawned lazily, and excitedly anticipated the laundry, cooking and cleaning she had planned for the day, just as any GOOD wife and mother would.

'Mirror, mirror on the wall, who's the most Perfect Mother of all?' she asked, a little more smug, knowing what the answer would be. The answer it had always been since she had given birth.

'Why, most Perfect Calzone Highness, you are perfect on most days but, today, it is Diana, who is a thousand times more perfect!'

'Why, thank…bwah, what?' Adina stopped herself. 'Di…? Di…a…What…?'

She was so upset that she could not even say the name. Di-a-what? There was only one person! It must be the new mother who had just moved in NEXT DOOR to her. That MUST be her, with her SEVEN children.

'AHHHH!' Adina screamed out loud in frustration.

There could only be one course of action. She had to get rid of her.

That morning, Adina met her Morning Coffee Mummy Girls, and started sharing what she had seen of Di-a-what from her window. Di-a- what left food under the couch; did not moisturise her baby three times a day as recommended by the Society for Perfect Mothers; and, gasp gasp, she drank a little red cooking wine while she was cooking, despite breastfeeding. There was pandemonium. The rumours caught on and spread like wildfire, degenerating until women would whisper publicly, 'Look at Di-a-what!' After three days of this, Di-a- what was no longer seen at the supermarket, school or playground. Adina gave two fist pumps in the air, her perfect body not jiggling at all.

The next morning, she once again asked the Mirror the usual question.

'Mirror, mirror on the wall, who is the most Perfect Mother of all?' The question was asked very confidently this time.

'You, my Queen Adina, are perfect, down to your starched panties and polished gold watch, it is true. But, beyond your walls, Diana, with the Seven Children, is still a thousand times more perfect than you!'

Adina gave a screech of frustration and threw her mug of decaffeinated coffee on the ground. 'NO!' Adina yelled.

Then, unexpectedly, she smiled. She had hatched the most evil plan. She would ....drum roll...bake the most delicious apple cake for Diana as a 'welcome' to Bullshit.

A poisoned apple cake, no less.

Adina marched to her neighbour's house and knocked loudly on the door, a cake in one arm and her perfect baby in the other. There was a scream from a baby and the harsh yelling of a woman, as the door was flung open by two very dirty looking children, still in pyjamas. Heavens! Pyjamas - and it was already 7:30 a.m! This? A Perfect Mother? In a home that had Lego all over the floor, and laundry heaped to the side! Adina snorted. Diana probably didn't even separate her laundry.

'Hi?' the neighbour said quietly.

'Hi, I'm Adina and I live next door to you. This is my baby boy, Self-Righteousness Judgemental Competitive I am Better than Thou and your Children....?'

'Oh, these are my children: Trust, Self-Esteem, Confidence, Hope, Joy, Peace of Mind, and my baby, Self-Love.'

'I have baked you an apple cake to welcome you and your little family.'

'Huh... that's nice... I...' the neighbour was unsure of what she should say.

Adina ignored her, marched right inside, and embarked upon what she saw as her sacred duty to dispense parenting advice to Diana before killing her.

'Come on, come on. Oh dear, did Mummy give you some CEREAL? Oh no, no, heavens no, this sugary cereal is so bad. Let's turn off the TV. Oh no, no, I would NEVER let my baby watch any TV, EVER! That rots the brain: do you not subscribe to the Journal of Best Parenting? And a dummy...oh, that's a big NO for us. And if your child really felt secure with you picking him up all the time, you would not need a dummy! Oh my... and you feed your kids packaged food? And you went where? Happy Meals? Oh no, Self-Righteousness would never eat anything like that...'

When the neighbour looked like she was already close to death from this verbal whipping, Adina knew that the time to strike was now.

'Come on, let's have some tea with this cake. It's gluten, dairy, sugar, butter and egg free, and organic. It's delicious too. Oh, not to worry, I'll wash your "clean" cups again... Look at that water stains. I'll wash them... And I'll wipe your bench for you as well... Oh, it's no trouble, no trouble at all... Here, TRY the cake while I wipe your baby's face! Goodness...'

Adina shoved a piece of cake into Diana's hands, and watched her take a bite as she helped to clean Self-Love's face, which seemed to have more food crud than the local fast-food restaurant.

As Diana took a bite and swallowed, she collapsed to the ground, unconscious. Adina gave a huge whoop of delight.

She'd done it! She rushed home with Self-Righteous, and went straight to her Mirror.

'Mirror, mirror on the wall, now pray tell: just who IS the Most Perfect Mother of all?' The confidence was evident in her voice.

'You, my Queen, you are almost the most perfect of them all. But there is still Diana, who is a thousand times more perfect than you.'

Maybe the magic didn't work. Maybe Diana had woken up. Adina stormed back to the house next door. There, on the floor, Diana remained, dead. She was surrounded by her seven children, who had now died along with her, as that's really how parenting truly works. Adina counted: there was Trust, Self Esteem, Confidence, Hope, Joy, Peace of Mind and Self-love...all gone! So what went wrong? Adina was puzzled as she walked out of the doorway.

'I don't understand... I did get rid of her!'

Out on the street, approaching the house, was Diana's husband. He seemed anxious and was yelling out, 'Suzy! Suzy! Are you all right? You didn't answer your mobile... SUZY!'

'Suzy?' Adina thought to herself, 'That was SUZY? Who the hell is Diana then?'

All of a sudden, Adina burst out laughing. She knew what had happened. She would return her Magic Mirror to the Ye Olde Shoppe of Magic Mirrors tomorrow and demand a full refund. Thank goodness it was still under warranty, as she had only bought it two weeks ago, a present to herself for giving birth to the Perfect Child. No, no, no, even better, she would use the refund and upgrade to the Ultra Mega Magic Mirror, guaranteed to last the whole lifetime of a child. And, even if there was a Diana, poisoned apples were always in season.

Adina was determined to be, as she is and will always be, the Most Perfect Mother in Bullshit.

AUTHOR BIO:

Michelle Tan is the absurdist comic writer and certified life-nonsense expert behind *"Ms Awesome, Mother Extraordinaire"*, the Facebook Page about surviving parenthood. Some call her genius, some call her dribble and some, like her three children, just call her "Mummy."

The Toddler Highway Code

Toddlers, of course, spend a lot of time on the move. As such, they have needed to formulate a set of rules for navigating the busy toddler thoroughfares of the living room, bedroom, garden, park or soft play. Toddlers police their Highway Code themselves. Enforcement is by means of shouting and foot-stamping. Penalties for non-compliance are usually in the form of a shove.

The Toddler Highway Code

(Applicable to all toddler roads and pathways. I.e. anywhere a toddler is choosing to toddle at any given moment.)

1. Right of Way
     Under toddler road rules, a toddler has right of way at all times. As does everybody else. This rule has been criticised for causing chaos and numerous small child pile-ups. However, the toddlers refuse to consider any amendment: they are too busy all running at once.

2. Give Way
     Under no circumstances should you ever give way. The presence of other toddler road users, cats, baby siblings or tables in no way negates this rule.

3. Lane Control
     Weaving is favoured. Lanes should be changed as

erratically as possible. As should direction. Ploughing into oncoming traffic (i.e. baby siblings) is encouraged.

4. Checks Before Manoeuvring

It is very important that you do not, under any circumstances, check behind you before performing a manoeuvre. Do not check in front of you either. If at all possible, perform the manoeuvre with your eyes actually closed.

5. Crossings

Crossings are neither acknowledged nor respected in the Toddler Highway Code. All persons attempting to cross the path of a toddler do so at their peril.

6. Parking

The basic toddler parking manoeuvre of sitting on your bottom should be performed suddenly and in the middle of the thoroughfare.

7. Acceleration

Acceleration towards all walls and other hard objects is encouraged.

8. Braking

Should be sudden and for no apparent reason.

9. Overtaking

The aim here is to overtake in the most dangerous, impractical manner possible. Close overtaking of wobbly baby siblings is approved. Overtaking in doorways, narrow spaces and on corners is ideal. Elbows should be used wherever possible.

10. Distractions

Proper toddler passage should be accompanied by as many

distractions as possible. Phone use, wand waving, talking, and having a basket on your head are all encouraged. Under no circumstances should you be looking where you are going.

It should be noted that it is usual practice to be screaming at all times during toddler transit. The toddlers would like it to be known that this is in no way a reflection upon the reasonableness or safety of the Toddler Highway Code.

AUTHOR BIO:
Lucy Gaskin is a mother to two young children.

Eating Out, Toddler Style

I'd love to eat out like a toddler.

I'd find it incredibly fun

To rock up in some fancy restaurant,

And act like I'm aged about one.

So first I'd object to the seating:

'I shan't sit in that, my dear friend!'

I shall thwart your attempts to persuade me,

By flat-out refusing to bend.

And then I shall grab for the menus,

A knife, and whatever I can.

'Til my table is cleared of obstructions,

And my food space is empty – good plan!

My meal shall be duly presented.

I shall cautiously give it the eye,

Then loudly announce, 'It is yucky!'

Without even having a try.

I'll reach out with one grubby finger,

And poke it to see if it's dead.

Then pick up my fork and lean over,

And pinch someone else's instead.

My chips shall be sauce applicators

For shovelling ketchup at pace.

I'll guzzle down half of the bottle,

Then rub the rest into my face.

I'll carefully pick every pea up,

And launch every one on the floor.

Then point at the ground in frustration,

And whinge until given some more.

But if I'm not keen on the green bits,

I'll blow raspberries and spit them all out,

And watch as my audience stifles a grin,

And one of them tries not to shout.

I'll pick up a gravy-soaked sausage,

And place it with love in my hair.

Then grin at the (silent) next table,

Whilst I try to escape from my chair.

I'll just bide my time until ice cream.

Then frantically bash with my spoon,

And shovel it in with distinct lack of grace,

Shouting, 'Om nom nom nom!' like a loon.

There shall not be time for a coffee,

I'll want to immediately leave.

Waiting for bills is just boring,

I shall freak like you wouldn't believe.

And as we abandon the restaurant

(For which someone else had to pay),

They'll get home all stuffed, stressed

and grumpy... 'Mummy, I hungry!' I'll say.

AUTHOR BIO:

Dawn White is the incredibly proud, thirty *mumbles* year old mum of two very busy children. Miss Tot is three and Master Tot is just one. They live in Yorkshire with their wonderful dad, her lovely hubby, who is fondly known as 'Daddy Pig', as he is of course 'rather an expert at everything'. The last three years have been mind-blowing, if a little bit mental. Her blog, *Rhyming with Wine*, is an ongoing collection of rhymes about the general silliness & hilarity of their family life. Her blog is named *Rhyming With Wine* because, well, 'whine' rhymes with 'wine', in much the same way as 'tantrum' rhymes with 'vodka' and generally most things rhyme with 'cake'!

Pre-Schooler CV

Personal Details

I'll get straight to the point: I'm looking for some gainful employment. Like many three-and-a-half-year-olds, I have time on my hands and skills that demand to be shared. And my parents would enjoy the peace and quiet afforded by my being out of the house for a few hours a week.

Opening Statement

New to the job market. I am one motivated, determined and focussed individual when it comes to achieving my own very specific goals. These may not be the same as your goals, but my positive can-do attitude (whilst not always entirely welcome) will astound you.

Educational Background

Don't be fooled by my young age: I may only have a minimal amount of what could loosely be termed 'education', and have spent only a few short years at the University of Life, but I have invested my time wisely. My borderline obsessional interest in a diverse range of subjects has been lovingly nurtured at home. My endless demands to read my favourite (completely age inappropriate) non-fiction books have led to the sort of in-depth knowledge that can take strangers rather aback, and frequently does.

Job History

Often to be found wearing realistic role-play clothing, and

with a vast range of props that are extremely convincing (at least to me), my work experience has taken many forms.

6.45-7.30 am: Doctor

Various family members were reassured by my caring, gentle and completely non-threatening manner with a syringe and a small hammer. I struggled to find their heartbeat and dispensed medicines with the sort of confidence that only comes from at least half an hour's experience in the field of medical practice and a tenuous understanding of the term 'budget cuts'. Such is my versatility, I also manage to act as a vet for the unsuspecting family pet.

I have a lift-the-flap Human Body book, and I am not afraid to use it. Although I do have some pretty terrifying misapprehensions, I have never been known to let being wrong put me off adopting an air of authority, and I am excellent at asking impertinent personal questions that really help to get to the bottom of things. Despite my encyclopaedic knowledge of the human body, please do remember to write my name on my scrubs. I might know all about the renal system, but I cannot always be expected to remember where I left my trousers.

8.20-9.05 am: Shopkeeper

After a short career break for breakfast, most mornings I am to be found setting up my very own department store. This sells all types of goods, including baby sisters, small valuables belonging to my older sibling, and free gifts that came with a magazine I got several months ago, which have either been broken or chewed beyond all recognition. All of these must-haves can be purchased from me at a cost I arrive at arbitrarily, and which bears no relation to their actual value.

My customer service skills are impeccable, and my sales

technique is best described as 'relentless', like a candidate on The Apprentice with a poor track record and an ambitious target. I take payment in imaginary coins or high fives, which has contributed to my excellent emergent maths skills, but if you run out of those, real money is also acceptable. However, be warned: retailers who are as busy as me cannot always guarantee to find the time for both service and a smile.

9.08-9.25 am: Busker
Before my main caregiver is able to convince me to get dressed, I spend a short spell as a musician, singing the classics at the top of my lungs whilst accompanying myself on the radiator, which makes an excellent substitute in the absence of a real piano. I am wasted in this bathroom: no one appreciates my obvious talents!

I excel when it comes to improvisation around a theme, coming up with my own lyrics being a particular strength, although they do all tend to have a scatological basis. Whilst it makes me laugh my head off, some of my audience are not very impressed. Tough crowd.

9.45-10.20 am: Town Planner
After a brief hiatus, during which I am wrestled into my clothes and groomed perfunctorily and against my will, I return eagerly to the world of work. Emptying my wooden train set, Lego collection and an assortment of vehicles onto my town play-mat may look like a mess to you, but I am busy creating a masterpiece that doubles handily as an obstacle course for anyone else with whom I am sharing my workspace.

10.35-11.20: Artist/painter and decorator
Next, to exercise my flair for the visual arts with a solo crafting session. As an artist, I work in many media, and I am nothing if not prolific. Again, my benevolent streak rears its

head, but any efforts to enhance the living environment with my skills proves a thankless task, as my lovingly rendered illustrations are wiped unceremoniously off walls and furniture without so much as a thank you. I do stop short of decorating the carpet, as the mere mention of the vacuum cleaner has me running for the hills.

Specialist Skills
~~Stubborn~~ Tenacious
~~Unpredictable~~ Creative
~~Problematic~~ Problem solver
~~Obstinate~~ Determined
~~Bossy and demanding~~ A born leader

Other Interests
Running, getting up at the crack of dawn, selective hearing.

References will not be provided unless bribed.

I hope you can see from this brief synopsis just how productive I am capable of being. All of this endeavour and it's barely even lunchtime.

AUTHOR BIO:
Alice Hanby is an avid crafter, reluctant fool-sufferer, can't-stop-maker, child-juggler, aspiring grammar pedant, book lover, and puzzle geek. She drinks far too many caffeinated hot drinks, and makes up stupid words for her own amusement. Her brain loves pointless information, so here is some for yours: she loves talking to strangers and she usually finds that this works out for her; she fell off her bike in 2000 and hasn't got back on; she had her second baby in the hospital car park; and she is the unfortunate beneficiary of her father's sense of humour.

Checklist: Is Your Child Gifted?

*Disclaimer: These questions are not scientifically proven to give any valid result, and do not guarantee your child entry to the best private school in the land. Sorry about that.

Most, but not all, of the following questions apply equally well to children of various ages. No one child will exhibit all of these. They are intended to serve as a checklist of the abilities revealed by many gifted children.

Please answer the following questions honestly.

1) **Did your child walk and talk earlier than most other children of his age and gender?**
   No. But he did crawl backwards for about a month... like a baby moonwalk. Michael Jackson would have been very proud of it.

2) **Did your child show a comparatively early interest in words?**
   Yes. Mainly interested in 'Peppa Pig!', 'Juice!' and 'Chocolate!'

3) **Did he have an exceptionally large vocabulary for his age?**
   Yes, but only when he's having a tantrum. He really is quite eloquent when he's fired up. Things that can cause outrage in a child are when *Peppa Pig* has finished or

when he wants crap food.

4) **Did he show an early interest in clocks, calendars and jigsaw puzzles?**
Yes. He learnt that clocks are very useful things for grown-ups to use in order to stop them from getting cross. Clocks can prevent the grown-ups from shouting phrases like 'get the hell up!', or 'we're chuffing late again!' As such, he does like to hide my watch, and he also resets the alarm clock every now and then so that the time is wrong on it, in order to keep me on my toes.

He likes jigsaw puzzles very much. The way the layers of paper they're made from can pull apart is very interesting, and they must taste really quite delicious (kind of like a Ryvita, I imagine) as he's always chomping on them. They must have some nutritional benefit, surely?

5) **Did he show an early interest in numbers?**
Yes. I think he does, as he seems to love seeing the numbers 2, 3 and 4. He wakes up to see them showing on the clock most nights, just to get his 'favourite number fix'. Yawn.

6) **Did he show an early interest in reading?**
Yes, again! Mainly newspapers and broadsheets. The noise they make when you stamp on them, and the mess you can make by ripping them up, are some of his favourite things to do. He also likes to rip the pages out of books. I think this is to alter the version of events in the story, and is particularly helpful if he's decided he's bored of the same outcome each time we read something.

7) **Does he express curiosity about many things?**

Yes. Mainly how his pee comes out of his winkle, and what happens when you flush a toilet. He's often found posting items down it and watching them 'magically disappear' when he pushes the special button. He also likes playing with food and transferring contents from once container to another, like cereal from his bowl into my candles. That sort of thing.

8) **Does he have more stamina and strength than other children of his age and gender?**
This is a yes. He can wrestle me onto the ground in a matter of seconds, and can go all day with very little sleep. It would appear that he only requires four hours sleep at the most per each twenty-four hours. He can also run like Roadrunner for a good length of time if mummy is shouting, 'Stop!' His endurance is really quite splendid. Puts Forrest Gump to shame, that's for sure.

9) **Does he tend to associate with children older than himself?**
Yes. He loves playing with his older siblings, especially games like 'Sit on Their Heads', and 'How Many Times Can I Get Away With Hitting Them Before Mummy Loses Her Shizzle'. He rarely leaves them alone, and he is stuck next to me (his mum) for approximately twenty hours of the day. I'd say he's a real people person.

10) **Does he act as a leader among children of his own age?**
Yes. He is really bossy (doesn't get that trait from me, of course) and, if he's not listened to, he may perform a martial arts move, such as a chin hold, on you until you agree to partake in his choice of activity. He has marvellous powers of persuasion.

11) **Does he have a good memory?**
He certainly does. He knows exactly where I've hidden

the special Christmas chocolates; and he's also brilliant at remembering all the things I've told him not to play with (dishwasher, DVD player, makeup, scissors, etc.), so that he can make a conscious effort to seek these things out.

12) Does he show unusual reasoning power?

Very much so. I think he has Jedi mind powers. Just one look can render me utterly powerless, and the biscuit I'd just said he couldn't have often finds its way into his hand.

13) Does he have an unusual capacity for planning and organising?

Yes. He plans his nightly wake-up schedule quite far in advance. He pushes me until he sees that I'm at point break and about to have a nervous breakdown due to sleep deprivation, then he will sleep through that night so I can regroup myself before the cycle starts again.

14) Does he relate information gained in the past to new knowledge he acquires?

Yes. He has figured out how to eject the drawer on the DVD player and put it away again. He also knows that small items, such as small bits of cereals, fit into small spaces. Therefore, the past information of the DVD drawer opening and closing has been added to the new knowledge of small things fitting in small spaces, and he has now put the two things together. Incidentally, it turns out DVD players don't like cereal much.

15) Does he show more interest in creative effort and new activities than in routine and repetitive tasks?

Yes. He is very creative. He often partakes in unusual creative activities, such as modern art. Our latest creation was called, 'Coffee by Candlelight'. We are entering it for the Turner Prize this year and believe he stands a good chance of winning, as he's up against a broken plastic garden chair and a cow pat set in concrete.

16) Does he concentrate on a single activity for a prolonged period of time without getting bored?
Yes. He can scream for at least two hours without stopping. Again, his stamina is something to behold.

17) Does he usually have a number of interests that keep him busy?
Yes. Making a mess with food, making a mess with drink, making a mess with toys and making a mess with dirt from the garden. He also likes having at least two tantrums a day: they take up a bit of time.

18) Does he persist in his efforts, even in the face of unexpected difficulties?
Oh yes. No amount of shouting, pleading, crying, blood offerings, bribery or promises of money from myself will stop my toddler from doing what it is he's set his mind to. He's not a giver-upper.

19) Does he have a sense of humour that is advanced for his age?
Yes. A sadistic one. He likes to see me shout and lose my s**t for his own personal pleasure. I'd say that's pretty advanced...

20) Does he make up stories that are vivid and dramatic, or relate his experiences with a great deal of exact detail?
Yes. But, sadly, we can't understand most of what he's saying or doing. It's very contemporary, interpretive stuff. We do know, however, that most stories involve 'Mumma, Dadda, Gray-gray, Nan-nan, Grandad and Peppa Pig'.

So, here endeth the questions.

What have we been able to deduce, I hear you all ask...

Well, in conclusion, based on the above answers, my child is 100% genius.

Who knew? I certainly didn't.

AUTHOR BIO:

Gemma Nuttall is a married mum with three boys, and lives in the UK. She writes a light-hearted blog called *Life Is Knutts*, which covers funny parenting anecdotes, cocktail & baking recipes, and day out/holiday write-ups. Everything to get you through parenting, cake, alcohol and humour.

The Green Food Strike

My kids are pretty crap picky eaters. That's right. As a mother, I have failed to make vegetables fun or fruit smoothies that actually taste good. So it won't surprise you to find out that The Kid won't eat any vegetables, and only eats bananas, pears and apples.

Whoops.

So, when The Baby came along, I lived in hope that the allotted fruit and vegetable gene distribution would be kinder to me this time and start dishing out some love. No such luck.

And so it pains me to say it, but we've been having a 1 in 3 success rate with The Baby's green to beige plate ratio, which of course, only means one thing. Both Spratts are going to get scurvy, and have mutant babies of their own.

But why? I did everything right. I weaned them on gag-inducing pea puree and chip-shaped sweet potatoes. (Okay, and the odd bit of cheesy pasta bake and Wotsits.)

If only I could ask them what the hell was going on in their crazy brains right now.

Me: So, er, I was wondering, girls, why don't you eat any fruit and vegetables anymore?

The Kid: I hate anything and everything green, Mummy. Except for green ice lollies and play-doh.

The Baby: What she said. You know how it is when you're two years old. Why put food in your mouth when you can try a table leg or part of Daddy's belt?

Me: Most other kids at least eat fruit, you know…

The Kid: Those kids are weak.

Me: Eating all of your fruit and vegetables will make you grow big and strong. Like Daddy.

The Baby: Screw Daddy.

Me: Most baby books suggest that…

The Kid: Hate books.

Me: …you should eat at least five fruit and vegetables a day.

The Kid: Goodness, woman! Get a grip! We aren't eating anything that looks green, purple, orange or red. Maybe even yellow if the feeling takes us.

Me: You'd feel a lot better if you did, you know.

The Baby: And you'd feel better if you just stopped banging on about it. Also, all this 'Here comes the fire engine' in that twat of a voice makes you sound like a dick. Soz.

Me: I wish someone would cook ME healthy meals…

The Kid: Here we go again…'boo hoo for you'. If you don't stop complaining, then I'll stop drinking those smoothies Grandma makes too.

Me: Alright, alright, let's not be too hasty here. I was just commenting that at three and two…

The Baby: Oh cut the crap, lady. We know your game here.

Me: I don't know what you mean, sweetie?

The Kid: Yeah. We see you nervously clutching your phone, ready to Google 'How to get my kids to poo quickly' again. I haven't been for three days now! Go me!

Me: I know, darling. We can smell you from a mile away. See, if you just ate your veg… And, anyway, you make Googling sound like a luxury!

The Baby: Well, isn't it?

Me: Er, yes, but…

The Kid: What's your game plan here? Hoping we both take a shit before we get in the car? Or are you bored of the twenty-minute toilet musical statues I make you play?

The Baby: Or my sudden need to wriggle my legs

uncontrollably?

Me: I'm only ever thinking of you two!

The Kid: Well, I'm not eating anything that isn't beige and covered in ketchup.

The Baby: And don't bother trying to grate them all up or hide them in spag bols. I'll just go mental, and chuck the cutlery at my sister and throw myself out my chair again. Try explaining that away to A&E this time!

Me: Okay...

The Kid: So let us make this crystal clear for you. We eat all kinds of food for Grandma, including mashed stuff. We don't eat anything that looks or smells healthy at home. ESPECIALLY if you've spent an hour cooking it. Got it?

Me: Well, sort of, yes, but, er, I was wondering if you would be so kind as to switch it round every so often?

The Baby: No. Well, now that's sorted...

The Kid: The park!

The Baby: But I wanted soft play...

The Kid: I SAID THE PARK!!!!!!!!!!!!!!!

Me: Sweethearts, it's the weekend and blowing a gale. We're going to be flipping cold at the park and I hate soft play.

The Baby: Shoes. On. Now.

Me: FFS

AUTHOR BIO:

Laura Suzanne Light is a mum of two small girls and currently (properly) under the influence of no sleep. She set up 'The Unsung Mum' one night after franticly Googling mum sites to check if she was as crap at being a mother as she thought. So, after blending her Gina Ford parenting book, she decided to set this site up to empower mums and remind them that they aren't cack. At all.

Where Do Babies Come From?

The Big Questions

I thought I would be a no-nonsense mum when it came to the 'awkward' or 'embarrassing' things that my children would ask. The big questions. I admire those mums who use the correct words for body parts, I really do. But I can't say penis without giggling.

I completely understand the argument that we should be upfront and honest with our kids. We should be grown-up about it. But! When The Big One asked me what girls have instead of willies (yes, we call them willies in our house), my brain went into panic mode. Seriously, there were alarm bells screeching in my head, and a million thoughts zooming around, all trying to be heard over the racket:

Don't call it a noo-noo.
What do other people call it?
This is going to affect the rest of his life. No pressure!
Seriously, don't call it a noo-noo.
Why is he asking ME this? Why can't he ask his father these questions?
Is he too young?
I'm sweating.
Vagina is the way to go.
Okay, you've totally got this.
No noo-noos around here.
Vagina, vagina, vagina.
Deep breath....
'Girls have a front bottom, darling.'

Face palms. You are such a noo-noo.

To be fair, I think I've gotten away with avoiding this question for quite a while with rapid subject changes. Most of these conversations have unsurprisingly taken place when I am accompanied to the toilet:

'Oh no, Mummy! Your willy fell off.'
'No! Mummy doesn't have a willy.'
'How does the wee come out?'
'Would you like some chocolate?'
'Yes please, can I eat it in the lounge and watch TV?'
'Of course.'

See, nicely avoided. Perfect parenting by anyone's standards.

Some questions I thought I was prepared for. When I was pregnant with The Little One, I assumed the 'Where do babies come from?' question was inevitable. The husband and I even discussed what we would tell him.

Except he didn't ask. The months ticked by, my stomach grew bigger, and there was no mention of how the baby got inside Mummy's tummy. Nothing!

But then one day he asked, 'Mummy, how is the baby going to get out of your tummy?'

Damn it. We hadn't prepared for that one.

When he eventually did ask the big question, a few months ago, I gave him the rehearsed answer.

'Daddy planted a special seed in Mummy's tummy.'

Given he is a six-year-old boy, and one of his favourite pastimes is running around the playground with his mates shouting 'BUM', 'POO' and 'WILLIES', less information is definitely more.

Except he had more questions. Damn it.

'Where did Daddy get the seed from?'

Shit! Why didn't we prepare for more questions?

'It's a special seed you get when you are a grown-up to make babies.'

Nice one!

'So how did Daddy put the seed inside your tummy?'

Seriously kid, what's with all the questions? What are you trying to do to me?

'Er, ummmm, Daddy gave Mummy a special cuddle.'

'Oh.'

OK, you've got away with it. Nicely done.

'Did Daddy put the seed up your bottom?'

*Hides face in kitchen cupboard, whilst laughing uncontrollably. (And, no, he most certainly didn't, just in case you are wondering!)

I am actually learning things from him at the moment. The other day he told me he had a 'widgie'...

'Do you mean a wedgie?' I asked.

'No, a widgie. Do you know what a widgie is?'

'No.'

'It's when your willy gets stuck to your balls.'

So. Now I know.

I can handle the questions about death, bad people and sad things. I can administer hugs and reassurance, no problem. But when it comes to body parts and sex, it turns out I am far from a no-nonsense mum. But that might be a good thing.

Last week we were in the queue at the supermarket surrounded by old ladies when he said, 'Mummy, I love my little brother so much'.

Cue lots of 'ahhs' from the surrounding bystanders.

'I'm so glad Daddy gave you that special cuddle.' Ahem.

I still think it sounds better than a six-year-old saying 'I'm so glad you and Daddy had sexual intercourse.' And way better than 'I'm so glad Daddy put his special seed up your bottom.'

I'm hoping by the time The Little One starts asking the big questions, I'll have all the answers. Failing that, I'm resorting to, 'Ask Daddy.'

AUTHOR BIO:

Claire Kirby is a self-confessed chocoholic and Gerard Butler enthusiast. She lives in the South of England with her husband, her seven-year-old son who never ever stops talking, and her two-year-old son who never ever stops moving. They live in a Lego house. They don't really, but they have so much of it they could probably build one. Claire writes a light-hearted parenting blog about life with kids: *Life, Love and Dirty Dishes.*

Why Can't We Have Sex Like The Coneheads?

Remember that amazingly outrageous movie starring Dan Aykroyd and Chris Farley, *The Coneheads*? If you are in your mid-thirties, like myself, then you might vaguely remember these alien folk posing as everyday suburbanites residing here on planet Earth. There is a scene in this movie where the teenage alien daughter and her boyfriend, Chris Farley, do the deed... but they are alien life forms, so it looks a bit different. They strap these contraptions onto their heads, bend their heads together so that they are lightly touching, and... BOOM! Orgasm. I will bet you ANYTHING a woman came up with this genius piece of scriptwriting.

Now that I am in my mid-thirties and have four small kids at home, I find myself thinking of this movie at least three times a week. I love my husband, I actually enjoy sex - or at least the effects of it - but I am so tired and lazy by the time sex 'o' clock rolls around, I want to bang like the Coneheads! Just bend my head towards my husband's head and have an earth-shattering orgasm. Truly, at this stage in the game, sexy time requires so much strength and endurance, yet I can barely muster up the energy to turn the page in my book at night.

I have already written about the three-times-a-week sexy rule. Less than that and I have a grumpy and useless husband. More than that... come on, no one does that! Here are the sexy time roadblocks that I find myself facing multiple times a week.

To shave or not to shave... In a perfect world, I would love to enter sexy time smooth as a baby's fanny, but in the real world it is shave or brush my teeth and wash my stinky, greasy mom hair. You can only have one, husband... choose wisely.

Nothing says sexy like mom jammies. Gone are the days where I strutted into the boudoir wearing an overpriced piece of lace and floss. Let us get one thing straight here: I am not spending money on that shit when I can buy three pairs of sweatpants at Target for the price of one negligee. Second, I am a little chubby and wrinkly now, and I am not feeling so sexy these days. My mom ass will swallow up a G-string like a fat kid with a piece of chocolate cake. Sweatpants and t-shirt it is... every night. Take it or leave it... please, just leave it.

Let me get this straight... you want me to get fancy with you, hubs? Like, move around? Nope. It needs to be enough for you that I put the channel changer down. You better be quick like a rabbit with this lovemaking. I am tired, and the kids are gonna wake up in ten minute intervals all night long. Besides, I am pretty sure the *Real Housewives of New Jersey* are on right now. You have two minutes.

Let's talk position, okay? Whatever drunken pretzel position I was able to contort myself into years ago is a distant memory now. Please, dear husband, do not break my hips. If you snap them, we are all up shit creek. This life of ours is not wheelchair accessible. Be kind, (and quick... have I driven that point home yet?).

I am so tired. Soooooooo tired by the end of the day. I have lived ten lives today, I swear. This mothering is some hard work.

I know... I should be spontaneous and sexy and wild, keep the passion burning. I should be thankful that my husband still spends most of his days chasing me around like a horny teenager. I am grateful for his attraction to me... truly. The thing is, I have four kids under nine years of age, and a husband who works his ass off from dusk until dawn. Until someone comes up with a way for us to have Conehead sex, three quickies and sweatpants is gonna have to suffice.

AUTHOR BIO:
Kristin McCarthy is a SAHM (stay-at-home mother) to four unruly princesses, as well as a published author and freelance writer. When she is not busy raising her humans and vacuuming up all small toys in sight, she can be found at the trolling the local Target, or hiding in her laundry room, where she writes for *The Things* and *Baby Gaga* as well as her own snarky blog, Four Princesses and the Cheese.

Together Against PENIS

Since becoming a mother over four years ago, I have noticed a disease that is spreading through the worldwide parenting community at such an alarming speed that I don't think it is an understatement to call it an epidemic. From the UK to the US, Australia to Zimbabwe, this condition is so severe that it is threatening the very future of our planet and the people within it.

You may not know this disease by its name, but you will almost certainly have encountered someone who is suffering from it. Hell, you may even be living with it yourself. It happens so suddenly and so completely that, when the first symptoms are displayed, it is often too late. By then, nothing can be done.

What is this disorder that has left me so concerned that I am stockpiling canned goods?

Known in Latin as "Parente Excludere Nihil Ingenium Syndrome" (PENIS), this frighteningly common ailment manifests itself as complete and utter humour loss as a result of parenthood.

It was first identified by Dr Van Wiener in 1973. Dr Wiener observed that monkeys at Berlin Zoo, who had recently given birth, were no longer laughing at other monkeys throwing their shit at visitors. It took nearly ten years before PENIS was recognised and granted disease status by the World Health Organisation. Even now, over forty years later, still very little is known about the exact cause of PENIS, but the consequences can be dire. And what's worse, is it highly contagious.

From the dusty Church Hall of your local playgroup to your whistles-and-bells Montessori Kindergarten, from doctors' surgeries to swimming pools: PENIS is lurking.

It doesn't discriminate. It doesn't care about race, gender, sexuality, religion, class or anything else, and it can, and it does, strike without warning.

Imagine never being able to take a joke or a witty aside? Never being able to identify sarcasm in the written word? Being physically unable to click through and read a whole article on social media, without finding yourself compelled to write an inaccurate, patronising and, quite frankly, bizarre comment? This is what sufferers, nay victims, of PENIS have to live with every day. What makes it worse is that they are completely and utterly incapable of recognising they have PENIS.

Sufferers like new mother Jane,* who, on the birth of her son Gideon, found herself unable to laugh at even the most obviously tongue-in-cheek comments.

'It started almost immediately after our little Giddy was born. I'd gasp at the odd comment at baby sensory, or tut at an overheard conversation in the library, and then another new-mum at an NCT coffee morning mentioned slipping some whiskey into her baby's bottle to help him sleep and I freaked out. I screamed and punched her in the tit before I ran out of there. I was shaking. I see now that these were the first tell-tale signs. Before long, I would trawl Mumsnet and Facebook for hours, looking for blogs and forum posts to comment on. I had no idea I had a problem: I thought I was just being a good mother but, by the time my family staged an intervention, I was commenting on upwards of a hundred Facebook posts a day. When my husband mentioned he thought I had PENIS, I didn't know what to think.'

Jane, who was voted third funniest in her year at the Sixth Form Leavers Dinner, and who used to love watching people fall over in the street, never thought that she would be diagnosed with fully-formed PENIS.

'I'm now expecting my second child and I'm petrified. My husband says I need to get a grip of my PENIS before the baby is born or else he'll leave me. But I can't, it's too hard,' she sobbed.

Unfortunately for Jane and the millions of other families across the world living with this wretched disease day in and day out, there is no cure. But I am determined to raise awareness of this condition so that people like Jane don't have to be ashamed. For too long its sufferers have been forced to live in the shadows, but I say 'no more'.

I've already gathered some big names working on this campaign with me: Jamie Oliver is writing a rap; Chris Martin is putting together some wanky black and white film with flashcards using Coldplay's *Fix You* as its soundtrack; Bob Geldof is starting to mobilise pop stars across the world for a global live concert so we can raise money to fund PENIS research and, one day, find a cure.

But we can't change things alone. We need you, PENIS-less and humourful parents of the world, to embrace this campaign and embrace those with PENIS. Together we can create a web of understanding, support, and one day, a cure for this truly terrible disease. Together we can thrust PENIS into the past where it belongs, and unsheathe those with PENIS so that one day they too can laugh again.

Peace, love and good humour, friends. May we never take it for granted again.

*Names have been changed to protect identities of all those involved

AUTHOR BIO:
Suzanne Treharne lives in Liverpool with her four-year-old daughter and seven-month-old son. She writes at '*...and another ten things*', where she attempts to explore the funnier

side of single parenting and smash the patriarchy one list of ten at a time.

Advice for New Parents (The kind you won't get from the child-health nurse)

When I fell pregnant with my first son, aged twenty-eight, I knew next to nothing about child-rearing. In all honesty, I wasn't entirely sure which way was up, so I made the executive decision to READ ALL THE INFORMATION.

I had no mummy friends, you see – no one to take me to one side and offer me the type of expletive-laden advice you don't find in the textbooks – so I dedicated the forty-three weeks of my son's gestation to reading about pregnancy, childbirth and beyond. Actually, I think that was the title of one of the books, since used for kindling. Because I can tell you how useful those textbooks turned out to be: NOT VERY BLOODY USEFUL AT ALL.

That's why, when friends of mine find themselves 'with child' these days, I offer them my decade's worth of mothering wisdom, whether they ask for it or not (they usually don't, but I tell them they'll thank me later). Think of this list as a public service, the type that money can't buy. YOU can thank me later, too.

1. Don't buy all the shit. You don't need all the shit. I made the mistake of going to a baby expo fair thing when I was pregnant with my eldest son, a decade ago. My god, the shit you could buy. The shit I did buy. You don't need all the shit. You definitely don't need fur-lined baby earmuffs.

2. Having said that, I found the following three things invaluable in the early days of new parenthood: a baby

sleeping bag, a breastfeeding pillow, and wine. They will tell you not to drink wine while breastfeeding. There are always ways around this. You can see me after class.

3. You will be told to write a birth plan but, once you have written it, you can forget your birth plan. The baby will have its own birth plan.

4. Take all the drugs you are offered (in labour). For the love of all things right and holy, take the drugs.

5. If you end up having a caesarean – and so many of us do – it's no big deal. The only thing that matters is the safe arrival of your precious baby. How she gets here is irrelevant.

6. You may be able to breastfeed. You may not be able to breastfeed. Big knockers are no indication of breastfeeding suitability. Some people simply aren't cut out for breastfeeding. If you are one of those people, then so be it.

7. If you do want to bottle-feed – by which I mean, if you want your life-partner to bottle-feed – then introduce a bottle fairly early on. People will tell you this causes nipple confusion (whatever that is). I don't know about that, but I do know that NONE of my three children would take a bottle – at ALL – and were attached to me by the bosom for far longer than is right or necessary.

8. Dummies are clever little inventions, aren't they? Neither of my boys took to a dummy, but my daughter has had one since day dot. The more she sucked on that, the less she sucked on me. Genius!

9. Get dressed every day. Sounds simple, no? It's not. But: get up, get dressed, go out (with the baby, ideally). Set yourself the tiniest of goals: post a letter, buy some milk, walk the dog. Yes, it will take you hours and hours and hours to achieve these teeny, tiny goals, but do them anyway.

10. Watch out for other mothers. If another mother – kindly – asks you if your daughter is 'sleeping through yet', ABORT MISSION IMMEDIATELY. Walk away. Reverse the pram and go home. The other mother doesn't give a shit if your

daughter is sleeping through. The other mother just wants to tell you that her daughter is. And she's probably lying anyway. Don't get involved.

11. On that subject: don't listen to other mothers. Don't listen to anyone. Especially old people. Everyone's an expert, especially in the supermarket. Have a baby and suddenly EVERYONE thinks they can tell you that your baby's too cold, too fat, too little, too hungry, too hairy, or too ginger. Ignore them all. Trust your instinct. Unless your instinct tells you to sit on the kerb in a bobble-hat shouting at passers-by. In which case, seek medical advice.

12. On a similar subject, don't read books. Specifically, baby books. I made the mistake of reading a how to put your baby to sleep book before my eldest's arrival. This messed me right up. Funnily enough, babies fly by their own rules, and aren't inclined to follow textbook guidelines. Your baby will do what he or she wants, when he or she wants. You can either go with it, or go insane.

13. Remember: you can't die from tiredness. Unless you're that Chinese dude who played PlayStation for two weeks straight, but he's the exception rather than the rule.

14. Finally, enjoy. Those few weeks after your baby's birth are precious and extraordinary and wonderful, although you might not realise it at the time. Spend time just looking at this beautiful, frog-like, possibly ginger, creature you created. Soak her in, and enjoy the fact that she can't wriggle around, climb bookshelves, talk back, and eat your Kit Kat (yet).

Those precious early weeks go way too quickly, so don't waste it worrying about milestones and other mothers.

AUTHOR BIO:
Mum-of-three **Lisa Shearon** is easily pleased – give her a chocolate-covered biscuit, a well-brewed cup of tea and an appropriately used apostrophe and she'll be yours for life. Lisa blogs at *The Notorious Mum*, and writes and edits at *Postscript*

Words. Word of warning: she's socially inept. If you meet Lisa, she'll ask how you are four times and then realise she's wearing odd shoes. Apologies in advance.

Just Call Me 'Secret Mum', Licensed to Change Nappies and Put You to Bed

Word on the street is that Her Majesty's Secret Service is having a BIG recruitment drive. Finally, my calling has come. I am here to serve my country and to protect it. Clearly, I am perfect for the job. I would make a super-spy! I am very confident that I will be recruited as their newest spy, Secret Agent Mum: the most resilient and determined of spies. I am so confident that you will soon be seeing me swanning around in some smart suit, whilst necking a martini, that I thought I would share with you my application letter.

Dear M,

I was recently on a very important mission. I had been tasked to get my children to school on time. A rival spy had noticed that our normal punctuality had slipped and, therefore, she had challenged me with a 'get them to school before the bell goes' mission. Otherwise known as, 'Is there anything we can help you with?' I was tempted to ask her if she could help prise my children out of the house when they are moaning that school is boring, and if she could somehow clear the road of traffic, especially old ladies who like to drive at ten miles per hour, and rampaging tractor drivers who are distracted by the Jersey Royals escaping out the back of their tractor. Instead, I gallantly bit my lip and accepted my mission. Therefore, imagine my delight when I heard on the radio that you required more spies. I fear that my time as a stay-at-home spy is coming to an end, and therefore, I would love to apply for this role. Here is why you should employ me as your spy:

- Blending in. As a stay-at-home mum I have perfected this art. In fact, I am practically invisible. Some days I am able to walk around detected by no-one.
- Extensive travel. I am used to travel. There is a saying on Jersey that, in order to stay sane, you must flee from the rock at least every three months. I can confirm that the saying is true. Once I did a gruelling six months and I nearly lost my marbles. I now try to leave/escape every other month.
- 'Going grey'. I am going grey. I blame the kids and Mr. C. However, I appreciate that going grey also means the ability to conceal your work from others. A-ha. I am very good at this. Mr. C seems to think that I spend my days swanning around and drinking coffee. Little does he know that I am actually carrying out research for my writing and blog. Obviously, that is why I spend my week working my way around the island's coffee shops.
- Keen observational skills. I have this nailed. I can tell if anyone has even opened the door to the sweetie cupboard. I can spy a toy from a 100ft, and my hearing means that I can tell when threenager is going to have a tantrum before she does.
- Good interrogation skills. This is an area of expertise. I have to frequently interrogate my children to determine who destroyed the bedroom, who ate the last chocolate biscuit, and what they did at school today.
- Persuasion skills. I am able to persuade Oldest to tidy her room by using several of my secret spy tricks, the most popular one being money.
- Spin a tale. A good spy can come up with a convincing story. Obviously, this is another area of expertise for me. Father Christmas, anyone? And let's not get started on the Tooth Fairy, and why she sometimes forgets (bad

mummy).

- Stealth mode. I can creep into the room of a sleeping seven-year-old, while navigating discarded Lego in the dark, and remove a tooth from under their pillow. *Cough* When I remember.
- Self-reliance. As a stay-at-home mum, I am very used to working on my own. It can be tough but we power on through.
- Can drive the get-away car. Have you tried driving a car with a threenager in the back launching toys at your head? I can drive under pressure. I am also very good at driving fast. Just say the words, 'I need a poo, Mummy!'

As I have outlined above, I think that I would make an excellent spy. I also have extensive knowledge of spies: I have watched all of the James Bond films and can confirm that Daniel Craig was your best spy. However, I am also partial to a bit of Inspector Gadget.

I look forward to hearing from you. Just remember the code words - 'But whhhhhhhhhhhhhhhhy?'

Yours
OO1 (because Mum is always number 1)

AUTHOR BIO:
Emma Critchley is a former teacher, who gave up life at the chalk face (okay, interactive white board face, but that doesn't sound quite as catchy) so that she could spend time with her own children. Emma now writes the award-winning lifestyle and parenting blog, *Island Living 365*. Emma is a self-employed freelance writer, who dreams about having her own magazine column one day, or a presenting job! She's not fussy. You can find Emma photographing Jersey on Instagram and wittering on twitter at *Island Living 365*.

Eight Women You Need to AVOID to Survive Mothers' Group

'Oh, I see that you've pushed a baby out of your vagina too. Let's be friends!'

Some of the more tedious aspects of motherhood are those situations where you are forced to socialise with a random assortment of other women based solely on the fact that you have all produced your own offspring. These include:

Playdates, playgroups, preschool.
Mothers' groups. Antenatal groups.
Breastfeeding meetings. Story time at the library.

They tend to be populated by people I'd never elect to hang out with in real life, so it can be a bit of a personality crap-shoot: some are boring, some are sanctimonious, some think Michael Bublé is the shit, and some are downright weird, but you don't realise it until you've been trapped in a conversation about nipple thrush for twenty-five minutes.

Here are the types you need to be wary of:

The Breathless Oversharer
Having finally escaped the solitary confinement of her infant-imposed house arrest, the floodgates of adult conversation are open – and nothing is off limits. You will be

hit with a tsunami of uncomfortable details about her health problems, her kid's health problems, her finances, her fractious relationship, her menstrual cycle, her sexual activity, and her thirty-six hour labour with forceps delivery. She doesn't get out much.

Talks about: Literally everything. You want it to stop but it never will.

The Neurotic Routine Mum

She is interested in your kid's sleeping habits in a way that is borderline creepy, lecturing you with the burning fervour of a fundamentalist. She is quick to mention that Little Johnny slept through at three weeks and credits her success to controlled crying and sleep gurus like Tizzie Hall. Her entire life is scheduled to-the-minute around her kid's eating and sleeping habits, and she is full of condescending pity if your baby still wakes overnight. Like a normal infant.

Talks about: The joys of self-settling, routines and controlled crying. Gasps in horror if you admit to 'going with the flow', bed-sharing, or feeding to sleep.

The Uptight First-Time Mum

Helicoptering madly, the uptight mum is easy to spot. She anxiously compares milestones, and can reel off quarterly growth stats from her child's first year. She has the health nurse on speed dial, and rocks up to emergency for minor bumps and scrapes. She can talk for hours about baby-led weaning, controlled crying and attachment parenting but is terrified that she is going to mess her kid up, because she hasn't done this gig long enough to know that we are going to mess them up no matter what we do, so it's not worth worrying about.

Talks about: Tomorrow's emergency doctor's appointment because Little Saffron has dropped down to the 97th percentile for weight.

The Absent, Free-Range Mum

You are doing well if you can even find this woman. She is never in eyesight or earshot of her children, who are usually the ones climbing six foot fences or falling face first off the playground equipment because a) her supervision is characterised by an excessively casual unconcern, or b) they aren't actually being supervised because she is nowhere to be seen. Stay away from her kids unless you are in a good position to catch them.

Talks about: Nothing, because she is never around. She might offer a cursory 'thanks' if you stop her children from scalping themselves on the merry-go-round.

The Milestone Braggart

Super-competitive, this Mum brags about the gifted child who smashes developmental milestones and is clearly superior in every way. 'Little Hugo was sitting SO much earlier than all of his peers.' 'Little Hugo could skip before he could walk.' 'Little Hugo was the first baby in my mothers' group to use coordinating conjunctions to connect two independent clauses.' And so on. She is not above making patently false claims to make her children look good. This kid even SHITS better than other kids.

Talks about: The perceived superiority of her child. Constantly.

The Overzealous Organic Mum

This 'hippy' mother is all about breastfeeding, baby-wearing, baby-led weaning, gentle discipline, and attachment parenting. She will roll her eyes at your Baby Bjorn carrier like it's an instrument of infant torture, and attempt to convince you that amber teething necklaces really work. Earnest to the point of sanctimony, she will react with horror when you reprimand Little Jasper for smashing his Tonka truck in Little Jimmy's face - again - because the little turd lacks boundaries.

Talks about: She will talk about baby carriers and cloth nappies until your eyes self-cauterise with catatonic boredom.

The Snarky Mummy Blogger

This woman had an identity crisis during a particularly inane craft activity and started blogging to fill the empty abyss where her life used to be. She blogs to indulge her wanton use of profanity, and to whine about her kids without giving them a complex that will one day require expensive professional intervention. She's always looking for new material, so your safest bet is to hide and, if cornered, sneer, 'Oh, so you're a MUMMY BLOGGER' with the same wearily disgusted expression you'd wear if you just stepped into a steaming pile of dog shit.

Talks about: Nothing. She's always listening for juicy snippets to use in her blog. Avoid her, unless you want your embarrassing exchange with Little Violet to go viral.

The Bitchy Gossiper

Perched at the centre of her own personal mummy clan, the bitchy gossiper is the reigning matriarch of her ice-cold clique. Like a high school mean girl, she controls social interactions by stealth and freezes out new mums until they have served a lengthy apprenticeship. Rude and dismissive, she ignores your polite attempts to make small talk – mortified by your ignorant breach of social etiquette. Stupid n00b.

Talks about: She's probably talking about you right now. You're such a loser. And your kid is ugly.

AUTHOR BIO:
Melissa Sorini is a wise-cracking mummy blogger with a Ph.D. in Snark. Famous for meat cake, piss-takes, and Thermomix-hate, she writes at *Hugzilla* blog: a celebration of imperfect parenting and gritty realities of modern motherhood.

The Egg Wars: A Little Tale of One-Upmanship and Parenting Judgement

Dinosaurs.

Come on, admit it, we all love them.

Our children wear clothes emblazoned with them, and carry around little plastic ones that they use to hit each other with. They stand in front of the television and demand to watch endless repeats of ANDY'S DINOSAUR ADVENTURES on CBeebies. They collect them in cereal packets, dance to big purple ones called Barney on American TV, and gawp at the real thing on show in the Natural History Museum. Even as adults, we revel in the words Triceratops and Velociraptor, even when we aren't entirely sure what they are or even if they were real.

We all know, of course, the story of how they died out; how sixty-five million years ago a meteor hit the Earth off the coast of what is now Mexico; but what if things had been different? What if the Chicxulub impact had never happened, and instead of the demise of the dinosaurs, followed by the rise of mammals as the dominant species, the dinosaurs had continued to flourish? The end result, I think, could have been something like this...

COSTA COFFEE, SOMEWHERE IN THE UK. FOUR DINOSAURS ARE AT THE TABLE, DRINKING THEIR MUMMY-LATTES AND GOSSIPING ABOUT LIFE AS A NEW MUM.

Velociraptor: 'Do you like my new shoes? I got them in the Next sale.'

Triceratops: 'Ooh, they're lovely. I must get a pair like that. Actually, well, is it a good idea to be wearing heels like those when you're carrying your baby in a sling? I mean, you might fall over or something. Don't get me wrong, I mean, like, your heels are FAB-U-LOUS, dahling, but you can't be too careful once you've got a little one, can you?'

Diplodocus: 'I'm surprised you've got time to go shopping, actually. What I wouldn't give for an hour or two to myself. You must have LOADS of free time if you managed to get to the Next sale. Our days are taken up entirely with swimming lessons. What with our family holiday to the USA next month, you just can't be too careful with the Western Interior Seaway covering most of the country. I couldn't live with myself if anything happened to Little Dipper. And then on Wednesdays we've got dino-sensory. How can I expect her to find her own leaves to eat someday if she isn't exposed to the feel of a branch on her face from infancy? Mr. Diplo and I have been fanning her with trees these last few weeks to get her used to the feel of a windy branch, but it's just not enough for her to learn these skills at home.'

Tyrannosaurus Regina (sic): 'That's why I've enrolled Mini-T in nursery twice a week. It'll help with his social skills.'

Diplodocus: 'Social skills? I'm not sure that your lot are known for your...'

Tyrannosaurus: 'What are you about to say?' *(Bares teeth)*

Diplodocus: 'I didn't mean anything by that. *(Swishes enormous tail, knocking over a family of smaller dinosaurs at a nearby table in the process.)* Anyway, I've got an appointment at the beauticians later.'

Velociraptor: 'Having your scales polished?'

Diplodocus: 'Yes. I just don't know how some mums do it, doing the school run in their PYJAMAS. I couldn't, personally. You've got to have a bit of pride. Even when things are falling apart at home, I make sure I've got my scales polished, my tail is neat and tidy, and I've got my lippy on.'

Tyrannosaurus: 'I know what you mean. Mr. T-Rex and I have standards. It's like in our house, we pride ourselves on being the king and queen of dinosaurs. Got to live up to the name, you know. The kids might be running riot and going around taking bites out of smaller dinosaurs, but the house is always tidy. I make sure there's not a carcass to be seen by the time Mr. T gets home.'

Triceratops: 'You might have a tidy house, but I hear that you were out hunting with Mr. T all through your pregnancy.'

Diplodocus: 'Really? I sat on my eggs for nine months straight. I couldn't have lived with myself if Little Dipper had been caught by any predators.'

Tyrannosaurus: 'Well, we ARE at the top of the food chain. We don't need to worry about these things.'

Diplodocus: 'We might be herbivores, but we know how to look after our young. There's just no substitute for a mother's love for a little one still in the shell. I can't believe anyone wouldn't sit on their own eggs. It's simply BARBARIC.'

Triceratops: 'I heard that you paid a couple of microraptors to sit on your eggs for you and keep them warm. Is that true?'

Tyrannosaurus: 'Look, we Tyrannosaurus have places to go, prey to hunt, other dinosaurs to terrorise. We can't sit there all day, twiddling our tiny arms, sitting on a bunch of eggs...'

Velociraptor: 'Well, in Mrs. T's defence, it's not just SITTING on the eggs that's important, is it?'

Diplodocus: 'What do you mean?'

Velociraptor: 'You know what I mean. Did you break your own eggs open? Or did you have, you know, HELP?'

Diplodocus: 'Those eggs were HARD! It would have taken DAYS to get them open. You can hardly blame me for using a hammer...'

Velociraptor: 'A HAMMER! What kind of mother breaks her own eggs open with a HAMMER?'

Diplodocus: 'We've got small arms!'

Triceratops: 'Personally, for me, the most important thing isn't how long you sit on your eggs, or whether you break them open yourself or let it happen naturally. What makes a great mother, for me, is someone who feeds their baby themselves.'

Tyrannosaurus: 'What, you mean, from your own mouth?'

Triceratops: 'You know what I mean. I fed Little Topper right from birth with regurgitated plants. Did you bring food home for your little ones, or did they have to fend for themselves?'

Velociraptor: 'I brought food home, of course. I might have brought home some of Little Topper's siblings, thinking about it.'

Tyrannosaurus: 'FEEDING THEM REGURGITATED PLANTS? What kind of Earth do you live on? One populated by mammals? No tyrannosaurus would feed that rubbish to their young, let alone regurgitate it directly into their innocent mouths. They need to learn that they are the kings and queens of the dinosaurs, right from an early age, and prey is there for the taking.'

Diplodocus: 'I wouldn't say we were there for the taking. We're massive.'

Tyrannosaur: 'I DIDN'T MEAN YOU! I wouldn't be sat in Costa having a Mummy-latte with you if I didn't like you.'

Triceratops: 'Why are we all having a go at each other then? Aren't we all trying to do the best we can, raising our young and hoping that they won't all get wiped out by an asteroid impact?'

Velociraptor: 'I suppose we are. Like Mrs. T said, I would have been eating you by now if I wasn't a friend. I don't even like lattes.'

Diplodocus: 'Well, there we are then. Let's all forget our differences and stop with this parenting judgement. We all do things our own way, and that's fine. We are all different species, after all.'

Tyrannosaurus: 'And how do we know that one day, a huge asteroid won't hit the Earth and wipe us all out, and all that will remain our fossils. And a few scale models, in a museum.'

Velociraptor: 'I wouldn't mind being a model... is remember what I was telling you about those heels?'

AUTHOR BIO:

Elaine Cogan is a single mother by choice, who finds herself in her mid-thirties and living with her mother again, like an overgrown teenager. She works full-time, writes an occasionally humorous blog, and enjoys collecting shoes. You can keep up to date with Elaine and her exploits at *http://www.singlemumspeaks.com.*

Beauty in to Beast (A Parody)

Like for many little girls, Belle was always the Disney princess I aspired to be. Beautiful, intelligent, thoughtful, and kind. Let's not forget that amazing dress, and the fact she got her Prince Charming in the end. Well, after a miraculous shave and a crash diet, of course. I can't help but wonder what Belle would have been like after she had been married to the Beast for five years, with two little mini Beasts in tow.

Disposing of poopy nappies was not the fairytale Disney princess life Belle had expected.

So, in true Disney style, below is my interpretation (with a bit of a Yorkshire twang) of Belle's song with a more realistic angle. Feel free to sing along.

Belle:
Little house, in a quiet village
Every day like the one before
Little house, full of whingey people
Waking up to say...

Little Beasts:
Mummy
Daddy
Mummy
Daddy
Mummy

Belle:

There goes the toddler waking up, like always
The same old whines and moans to yell
Every morning just the same
At 6 a.m., mini beasts came
To see our poor tired parents frown

Beast:
Good morning, Belle.

Belle:
Good morning, Daddy, er, I mean Beast.

Beast:
Where are you off to?

Belle:
The shops: I need to pick up some strong coffee, nappies, wipes, milk and bread.

Beast:
That's nice. Can you get me some sandwich meats for lunch? LITTLE BEAST!! Stop poking me in the head.

Townsfolk:
Look, there she goes
The lass is strange, no question
Dazed and distracted, can't you tell?

Man:
Never part of any crowd.

Woman:
Cause her head's up on some cloud
No denying she's a mummy now, that Belle.

Man 1:

Ey up!

Woman 1:
Good day!

Man 1:
How is your family?

Woman 2:
Ey up!

Man 2:
Good day.

Woman 2:
How is your wife?

Woman 3:
I need... a Greggs.

Man 3:
That's too expensive!*
(*What Greggs?!)

Belle:
There must be more than this abysmal* life!
(*Okay, so abysmal is a tad extreme, but I was struggling to find something to rhyme)

Man at the Library:
Ah, Belle.

Belle:
Good morning. I've come to return the kid's book I borrowed.

Man at the Library:

Finished already?

Belle:
Yes, I've read it to them at least a hundred times and they still aren't bored yet. Please tell me you've got something else?

Man at the Library:
Not since yesterday.

Belle:
That's alright. Okay then, we'll borrow this one (after an argument with toddler over said book, as it's not the right colour or size).

Man at the Library:
That one? But you've read it twice!

Belle:
What, 'Charlie Cook's Favourite Book'? Yes, it's my favourite. I like doing all the voices; my pirate and knight are especially impressive.

Man at the Library:
Well if you like it all that much, it's yours.

Belle:
Really? What, actually free? What's the catch? I mean, do you need my email address or something so you can constantly spam me?

Man at the Library:
No catch, I insist!

Belle:
Nice one, ta very muchly!

Townsfolk:
Look, there she goes, that lass is super-human
I wonder if she's feeling well

Men:
She seems a little snappy.

Women:
Because her nose is in a nappy

Townsfolk:
She needs to be an octopus, that Belle.

Belle:
Ewwww... isn't this disgusting?
It's my least best part of being mummy
Here's where I see the bogies
Crusting on my newly-washed leggings
On both my knees!

Woman:
Now it's a wonder why her name means 'beauty'
Her looks are fuelled on Zinfandel

Shopkeeper:
But behind that zombie plod
I'm afraid she feels a fraud
Very distant from the rest of us

Group of mums:
She's struggling like the rest of us
Yes, normal like the rest of us, is Belle

(The next part is traditionally sung by Gaston and Lefou but, for the purposes of this, it shall be sang by the beast and Trevor (yes I totally made that up), his best friend.)

Trevor:
Wow, you look knackered, Beast. Are you tired?

Beast:
I know, yes, I'm exhausted. I'm always working, the kids are non-stop, and Belle does not stop nagging at me.

Trevor:
Oh dear, it doesn't sound like the fairytale it used to be.

Beast:
I know. I still really love her, but she just seems to have lost her mojo.

Trevor:
Does she not still have that flouncy gold dress?

Beast:
No, she mostly lives in snot and food-stained clothes, and never wears matching bra and knickers.

Trevor:
But she was...

Beast:
The most beautiful girl in town? She was, but now she has more hair on her legs than I ever did.

Trevor:
That bad, huh?

Beast:
Yes, well, since she had the kids, I've been put to the bottom of the pile.

Trevor:
Go on then, tell me about it.

Beast:
Right from the moment when the kids were born
The trouser kisses were just shelved
Although I must agree
She makes a nice hot tea
So I need to re-woo and de-hairy Belle

Group of mums:
Look Beast, it's hard to be a mummy
Hey Beast, it's hard to be a wife
Give her a chance, she feels like screaming
It's not the perfect mummy kind of life!

Man 1:
Ey up.

Beast:
My bad!

Man 2:
Good day.

Man 3:
By heck!

Matron:
She's shoving cake in.

Woman 1:
You need some wipes!

Man 4:
Some nappies...

Woman 2:
...Two packs!

Man 4:
...Four pound...

Woman 1:
It's real life.

Beast:
There's too much poo!!

Woman 2:
My head...

Man 5:
Those kids…

Woman 2:
...They're cute

Man 5:
...They smell of hamsters.

Belle:
There must be more than this abysmal* life!
(*Once again, a bit harsh, and purely for rhyming slackness)

Beast:
I'm so proud to call lovely Belle my wife (even if she does look a bit of a bugger, and nags a lot).

Belle:
Life as a mum can be a little stressful
Often a challenge not to yell

I used to be quite slim
Pass the tonic and the gin
It's super being a mummy
Bar the wobbly wibbly tummy
Yes, I do love being a mummy...it's just swell (well, most of the time).

(And they all lived happy-ish-ly ever after.)

The End

AUTHOR BIO:
Colleyswobbles (aka, **Gemma Colley**) is a blogger from Yorkshire, England. She started her blogging journey after a rather crazy brush with viral fame, and wanted to reignite her passion for writing and creativity. As a mum to two very active boys, she often writes about trying to figure out parenthood whilst riding the wave that is life, wobbles and all.

Mummy Princess Goes to a Meeting

Once upon a time, in the Kingdom of Ealing, there was a Mummy Princess, standing in front of a bathroom mirror, crying.

Why was Mummy Princess crying? She was crying because she had stabbed herself in the eye three times with eyeliner whilst trying to apply make-up. Mummy Princess usually spends her days wedged on the sofa, eating crisps and watching Sir Jeremy of Kyle shout at the commoners, so she is not used to wearing make-up.

But today was different. Mummy Princess needed to look less like a Zombie and more like that other Princess: Kate Middleton. For Mummy Princess had a very important meeting to attend.

Daddy Prince had to take the morning off work in order to look after Princess Tantrum, while Mummy Princess swanned off to have 'fun'.

Yes, that's right, that awful Daddy Prince had called Mummy Princess' important work meeting 'fun'. This annoyed Mummy Princess so much that she gave Princess Tantrum a Yorkie for breakfast so that she would act like a thing possessed for Daddy Prince all morning.

'Sod you, Daddy Prince,' thought Mummy Princess, as she applied the eyeliner very badly, for the final time, not caring that she looked like a fat Goth after a messy night out.

'Be back in time for me to get off to the Kingdom of London, so I can do my proper important work that pays the bills for the Castle,' shouted Daddy Prince, as Mummy

Princess got in her carriage (which the nice people from the Kingdom of Uber had sent for her) to leave.

Mummy Princess flipped him the finger behind her bag.

"I really hate you, you self-important git," she mumbled.

"What was that?" asked Daddy Prince, a little too aggressively for Mummy Princess' liking.

"I said, 'I love you'," lied Mummy Princess, through gritted teeth. "See you soon."

The journey was very pleasant for Mummy Princess, as she had lots of time to think about all the ways she wanted to kill Daddy Prince, and all the superheroes from the Kingdom of Marvel she would try it on with once he was dead.

After having lots of lovely thoughts about Spiderman and Thor, the Uber carriage arrived at the big, sparkly building.

'Oh Jesus, we are here,' thought Mummy Princess, as she stumbled out of the car in a most unladylike manner, wishing that she didn't have a "No booze before lunchtime" policy. 'Surely, this would be much easier if I was slightly drunk.'

After getting caught in the revolving door three times, Mummy Princess successfully negotiated her way into the building. She smoothed down her unkempt, frizzy hair, which was now ruined as she had spent three seconds outside, and checked that her skirt wasn't tucked into her knickers. As she brushed the last few flakes of her sausage roll from her bosom, she announced her arrival to the girl on reception, who was young and thin, and made fat, old Mummy Princess irrationally angry.

'I bet that cow doesn't have children. Her clothes are too expensive,' thought Mummy princess, like the jealous, petty bitch she was.

After waiting ages and forgetting everything she wanted to say, Mummy Princess was called into the meeting by a big, fire-breathing dragon. This fire-breathing dragon was a very important person, with the ability to either make Mummy Princess a lot of money, or to ruin Mummy Princess in an instant.

It was very important that Mummy Princess impressed this fire-breathing dragon, as Mummy Princess' castle was a bit of a hole, and she would quite like another one that didn't have holes in the floor.

Mummy Princess followed the fire-breathing dragon into her office, trying not to fall over or do anything else that was stupid.

Unfortunately, Mummy Princess is stupid, and also rather clumsy, and as she sat down, she almost missed the chair and whacked her arse on the arms.

'For God's sake,' thought Mummy Princess, trying to smile instead of cry, 'seriously?'

It turns out the fire-breathing dragon had seen Mummy Princess before, at a party. When Mummy Princess heard this, she panicked.

'Oh no,' thought Mummy Princess, 'how drunk was I, and what was I saying? Who did I annoy? Oh God, I will never drink again.'

It turned out it was okay, because the person who Mummy Princess annoyed that night was someone who the fire-breathing dragon didn't like very much. Instead of thinking that Mummy Princess was just a loud drunk (which was true), she thought that Mummy Princess was funny, clever, and knew what she was doing (which was not true).

The fire-breathing dragon turned out to like Mummy Princess very much, and Mummy Princess signed a piece of paper to say that the fire-breathing dragon could have twelve percent of all the money she made.

"You'd better get me a shed load of work," said Mummy Princess, out loud this time. As she had now signed a contract, the fire-breathing dragon couldn't tell her to get lost.

The fire-breathing dragon took Mummy Princess out for a brunch with lots of booze. By the time Mummy Princess got back to her castle, she didn't care that Daddy Prince was a massive twat, or that Princess Tantrum had vomited chocolate over the cream carpets. She was just happy that one day she might make enough money to run away from them all.

AUTHOR BIO:
Cookie Kibbles is a comedy writer and ex stand-up comedian. Having spent years writing and editing behind-the-scenes for other comics, she is now writing her own blog, TV and radio shows.

The Play Date

Play dates, play dates, play dates - don't we all just love play dates?

They can go one of two ways. Refreshingly easy: the children disappear upstairs, all goes quiet, and you find them cutting each other's hair with your Lady Shave. Or completely stressful: you have to intervene every two seconds, as your child whinges 'Flora says my feet stink of cheesy Wotsits' or 'Cara says my mum is fat'. Hang on a minute, that would be me then... wtf?

So, I try to avoid them at all costs. But, of course, my children want them. All their classmates are playing at each other's houses after school, and my children have become the Boo Radley kids. They can hear the whispers in the playground: 'Nobody's ever been allowed in the house. Apparently, their mum and dad walk around naked, singing *In the Night Garden* songs.'

But we don't want complete ostracisation, so I asked my children in turn who they'd like to invite round to play. When I got to Eldest Child, she said the one name I was really, really hoping she wouldn't say. I had to admire her ambition though. She was aiming high. She suggested we ask Maisie, The Most Popular Girl in Class.

'Okay, no problem,' I said in a high-pitched voice. Why not? Let's think big. I'm sure she'll want to come to our little old house, if only just to tell the rest of the class that, indeed, Eldest Child's parents do walk around naked. Not while listening to the theme tunes of children's TV programmes, I hasten to add. No, no, no... We're more of a soft rock kind of a pair.

Now, trying to get a play date with this child is a mean feat in itself. I'm guessing she gets about thirty requests in one week alone, so you need to get in early to reserve a slot.

I managed to get a booking a few weeks in advance so, when the big day arrived, we were all ready for Marvellous Maisie to have the play date of her life. Oh yes, it was going to be so wonderful that she would surely be desperate to come back for more. We might even jump to the top of the waiting list next time.

I must just tell you at this point that it's plain to see why Maisie is the most popular girl in the class. She's got *that* hair. You know, that long, glossy, golden hair that everyone covets. It never looks messy, looks amazing in bunches, in plaits, in top knots, it might even get away with a mullet. And it's always tied up in gorgeous matching bobbles. Not scraggy elastic bands that have been found down the back of the sofa, but matching strawberries, or glittery love hearts.

But, apart from the hair, Maisie is actually a really lovely girl. She's everyone's friend. She's kind, she's sweet, she's not yet old enough to realise she's hugely popular, and can use this powerful tool to be a bitch and get everyone to do what she wants.

The big day arrives, and I've laid on a special spread of cookies and juice. Not only that, but I'm being all, 'Yay, just help yourself guys. Everything's cool in this house. It's the most fun house in the world.'

My children can't believe their luck. There is an alien woman in the house. She looks similar to the usual woman, but is, instead, calm, patient and even a little bit fun.

After their cookies (I notice Maisie delicately eats one, whereas my little gannets scoff three each), Eldest Child and her chosen one disappear upstairs.

I'm just preparing my freshly made spaghetti bolognaise - no chicken teddies and beans tonight - when I realise it's gone very quiet upstairs. I decide to investigate, assuming I will find them in Eldest Child's bedroom playing beautifully with dolls, as I imagine only Maisie does.

But hang on, what's that I can hear coming from my bedroom? There's a deep American voice shouting **** you, you *******', followed by various other not very child-friendly words.

Oh no, oh no! This can't be happening.

I run into our bedroom to find two little girls, huddled round my laptop, all agog as they watch some rude, awful, sweary clip on YouTube. This is terrible. How on earth has this happened? Why hadn't I ever got round to setting up Net Nanny?

I race over and slam the top of the laptop shut.

'For ***** sake!' I scream. They look at me aghast by my outburst. I quickly remember myself, and who we have in our presence.

'I don't think we should be watching that now, should we?' I squeak. 'Perhaps don't tell your mummy, Maisie. Why don't you girls come down for supper now? It's spaghetti bolognaise!'

My child looks at me, astounded. I know she's wondering where on earth the customary chicken teds are. I pull myself together after the shock of the YouTube incident, and glow with motherly pride as I dish up my homemade wonder. My kids are obviously looking at it as though it's a pile of dog poo, but lovely Maisie is wolfing it down, much to my delight.

That is, until her knife and fork suddenly clatter down on to the plate, and we all watch in horror as she pulls out a long black hair. She then gives a little retch. Who can blame her? That is utterly disgusting.

Everyone pushes their plates away in revulsion. Appetites have vanished. Maisie, bless her, gives a half-smile but looks like she might puke her load. I whip away the plates, and have to have a moment holding on to the sink for my blood pressure to reduce.

Could this play date be any worse? Will all the mothers at school soon know that I serve hairy food? At least it wasn't a pube – small mercies.

I give the children ice creams, which appeases the situation, and thankfully the disastrous tea time is over.

As the girls are happily playing in the living room afterwards, youngest Boy Child toddles in and heads straight for Maisie. We're all drawn to her. This most golden, glossy-haired child. I think he can sense she is the Most Popular Girl in the Class and, as a reward, he curls one out. Right there, on the floor, by her feet. Like an offering: 'I hereby present to you a big, fat, brown, stinky jobby, in recognition of your high status. Please don't be alarmed. It is merely in appreciation of all the work you do, in being so ridiculously popular.'

Maisie's face contorts with utter horror. I cannot believe that Boy Child has done this today of all days, at the feet of our most revered guest. She is retching again. Not even my speedy scooping up of the poo, whilst I tell her how beautiful her matching pumpkin bobbles are, can help the poor girl. She is traumatised.

The doorbell goes. It is time for her to leave. I have a feeling she won't be back. I have a feeling I will soon be known by all in the playground as the weird mother who allows her children to watch dodgy YouTube clips featuring the F word a lot, who herself uses the F word a lot, who serves up hairy food, and who thinks nothing of her children crapping on the living room floor.

Oh well, who needs play dates anyway?

AUTHOR BIO:
Susie Weaver lives in London with her husband and three

children. She is a writer and teacher, and now runs her own lifestyle and parenting blog called *So Happy in Town*. Her writing regularly features in *The Huffington Post*.

10 Rules of Hotel Etiquette

Lots of people get excited about hotels: if you don't have to stay in them all the time, they can be a treat, an opportunity to step out of normal domestic life and enjoy someone else's cooking and, I don't know, hoovering.

Having ventured to a few hotels with a not-quite-two year old, I realise that it's not only adults who can get giddy about these establishments.

Indeed, I've been observing my son's enthusiasm and his complete confidence in his own behaviour. It has brought me to the only conclusion I can find: I have obviously been showing myself up as a complete hotel ignoramus, and my grasp of hotel etiquette has been, up until this point, completely misguided. I don't want anyone else to have to suffer this unnecessary embarrassment, so please conduct yourself according to the following ten rules next time you find yourself within a hotel.

1. Fancy Details

Plush carpets... ignore. Sparkly, big chandeliers... ignore. Interesting artwork... ignore (unless it features cars, cranes, hovercrafts or lorries).

2. Familiar Faces

If you happen to be staying in a hotel where other people you know are also staying, it is fine to declare the connection 'daddy' (matching tracksuits are a giveaway), but then you must ignore them completely if they try to talk to you. Do they not know that we are *not* at home?

3. The Locale

Clearly, everyone else in the hotel needs reminding of where the hotel is situated. It is important here to really shout, and also point in the direction of exits: 'SEASIDE!'

4. Lifts

The instructions here are twofold. Pay attention. Firstly, it is imperative to repeat the lift voice, particularly 'doors opening' and 'doors closing'. You must then repeat this throughout the day, whether or not you are in the lift. Secondly, do you see the big yellow button with the picture of the bell on it? Yes? Good. You must try and press this button. You must spend the entire lift journey trying to press this button. If you succeed, and you probably will the first time as surprise is on your side, it will initiate a pleasing duet of ringing bells and mummy shouting.

5. Staff and Other Guests

There are a lot of people in a hotel, and not all will be familiar. It is only polite to acknowledge all of them in exactly the same way: point, wave and shout 'man'. If at any point they see this as an invitation for conversation, they are wrong and you should proceed to ignore them totally until they walk away. Then you can offer your 'man' greeting once more, to the safety of a retreating back.

6. Biscuits

The exception to the above rule is the person hanging out in the hallway with a trolley full of biscuits. Start out, as with others, by saying 'man' (fair's fair), then wait. If biscuits are offered, you can engage in small talk. Keep it simple though... perhaps just show them the tractor on your tummy. After that, run away with biscuits.

---

7. Hallways

You must never walk in a hotel. Do you know nothing? Run, always run. Keep running, and shout 'round the corner' loudly as you navigate bends.

8. Breakfast Buffet

Or, in other words, the all-you-can-eat breakfast buffet. A personal challenge to eat as much scrambled egg and baked beans with your fingers as possible. Remember that, unlike at home, it is never 'all gone'.

9. Tea Making Facilities

Listen carefully to this one, it's important... the person you are with may not realise they could make a cup of tea *and* sleep in the same room. It is your duty to remind them. Preferably when they are lying in bed, trying to sleep, at about 10:30 p.m. Do it loudly and make sure they understand exactly the wonder that is available to them: 'TEAPOT, TEABAG, CUP OF TEA'. Repeat if necessary.

10. The Bed

Hotel beds are big, but they shouldn't be allowed to get above their station. One bed = one pillow. Discard all others onto floor and recline. While we are on the subject, a big bed means there is clearly more than enough room for you and whoever the bed was meant for. Do not be fobbed off with a travel cot.

Finally, I urge you to enjoy every minute because, if you follow the above instructions carefully, you will probably not find yourself taken to too many hotels in the future. And, of course, don't forget to tip. We recommend a raisin and a piece of fluff.

AUTHOR BIO:
Lucy Tomlinson is a stay-at-home feminist mother just about

surviving life with a toddler. She blogs at *Occupation: (M)other* – not so much a lifestyle blog as a life-thoughts one. She took the digital plunge to vent some serious thoughts, make some feminist arguments and, obviously, change the world. Then she started writing and, instead, she mostly makes herself laugh, uses a variety of probably unorthodox sentence structures, and finds mildly quirky angles on life. So, in a digital nutshell, *Occupation: (M)other* - her award-nominated, award-shortlisted, but no-actual-award blog - bumbles along, changing her world and allowing her the lovely opportunity to unashamedly laugh at her own jokes.

Dear Neighbours in Our Apartment Complex

Dear Neighbours in Our Apartment Complex,

I need to clarify a few things for you all.

I believe you know of' me. You may be forgiven for thinking my name is something exotic, something quirky even. But that high-pitched 'MMMUUUUMMMYYYY' that you all no doubt hear being squawked all day is actually just my 'work' name. In fact, I am occasionally referred to as Anna, and, well, I'm guessing you know my kids' names. They are often shouted (on repeat) through your vents/walls from 6 a.m. (on a good morning) through until around 8 p.m. This is on a daily cycle. I try, I really do. But, people, the days are long and the walls are thin. Your anger is possibly on a par with my shame; this is high-density, apartment-style living.

We all made choices.

Let me walk you through a few little things that I need to make clear.

That smell that hit you for six when you stepped in the lift? It was us. I had to get those nappies downstairs somehow. How your heart must sink those times that the doors slide open and we are your lift buddies. Buttons are shiny and they do 'things'. I was interested to see the different layouts of each floor, weren't you? Fingerprints on the lift mirrors? Us again. In fact, the little one has a small obsession with licking those mirrors. Enough said.

There is an 'outside' voice. Then there is an 'inside' voice. But the 'apartment' voice creates a whole new set of challenges. Anything above a whisper and I am doing my *Anxious Anna* dance. I have a five-year-old and a three-year-old. I do not even remember what their 'whisper' voice sounds like. In fact, that constant 'SHHHHH' noise is not the hot water system: it is my persistent drone, all day long. Taking them outside is an excellent suggestion, and I do. But, neighbours, we have to live. It has also been winter; I work from home; and the 'getting them outside' bit sounds way easier than it is. Plus, we have been in toilet training lockdown. Bless us all, but I think we are on the other side.

And, of course, my kids need to eat. I confess: I am not a great cook. I present meals at the appropriate time (Look out for the tantrums if they are hungry. Oh yeah... you know all about those), I try to provide balanced meals, and I also try to serve food that my kids like. But, though sausages, rice and broccoli have pretty much become a staple here, it is generally still '**SCUSTING**!!' During every meal at the moment, the boy cries in agony at the thought of having to eat something so obviously and completely horrendous. He heads right to screaming, long and loud. And, yes, whatever you are thinking to suggest, it is likely I have tried it.

I also have a threenager. Please understand. She asks for Weetabix. I give her Weetabix. She then screams for toast. How could I (apparently) get it so wrong? *Obviously,* I am a mind reader with superhuman powers (only sometimes).

Dear neighbours, I do not want to raise a brat. I have to sit it out. I have to teach her appropriate behaviour. Tantrums, loud and long, are her latest accomplishment. Please believe I have not locked her in her room or left her alone. She screams that she wants her mummy, but will not let me go near her or comfort her. You sit in a room with someone screaming for up to half an hour and see how you go. If you hear me responding perhaps a little 'inappropriately' at some point, please forgive me. I know I have to be the adult here, but...

Then there are the 'good' screams. If wild wails meet you as you hit the foyer after work, please know that bath time in our house is actually a joyous and raucous occasion. Our bathroom wall adjoins this public space. Picture sharks, goggles, flippers and fountains. That screaming is, more often than not, actually pure joy. Consequently, my kids have long baths. Of course, that moment Daddy puts the key in the lock of an evening? I become invisible as the shrieks abound from all parties!

Oh, people, summer is coming. Our balcony doors are being pulled open more and more to let the fresh, healing, spring air inside. Of course, that means voices carry. Sometimes I can bellow back. I do. My patience is probably on a par with yours. You see, I do this all day, every day.

"I don't want that."
"That's 'SCUSTING!"
"Weeeee!!!"
"Pooooo!!!"
"I want to put on ANOTHER Princess dress."
"Wipe my bottom."
"She stole the red crayon."
"I hate carrots."

I chose this life. I did. But stay-at-home-mothers (who are also trying to squeeze in working from home, too) are allowed 'bad days', just like you, aren't they? I know you hear me. Just remember though: if you can hear me, sometimes I hear you, too.

Next time you see me struggling with shopping bags twisted around my purple fingers, or grabbing the jumper of a child who is making a bolt for the lift, or having a moment as I try to strap two wriggling kids in the car, please say 'hello'. You might also learn that my daughter genuinely thinks you see a Princess if she is dressed up, and my son is proudly learning how to write his name. I love writing and a buttery chardonnay, and my husband is passionate about cycling and his family. A smile or an offer of help can be all it takes to change my day around.

You see, please understand: we are so much more than just *those* people with the noisy kids.

Sincerely,
Anna

AUTHOR BIO:
Anna Brophy is an Australian teacher, mummy, writer, and blogger at *Mummy Muckups*, sharing her sparkling highs and challenging lows as a mum to two 'spirited' kids and the wife to her lycra-legged Husband. She writes the truth as she sees it through sleep-deprived eyes and a heart full of love. She is excited to be able to share with you one of her favourite blog pieces outlining the tough realities of apartment-style living when you have a five and a three year old. She sends a huge thank you to Michelle for having her along. Oh... and she also must make a special mention to sparkling wine... and crispy bacon... and salted caramel... who have provided her with unfailing support in her journey thus far.

Peppa Pig More Addictive Than Cocaine, Warns Expert

Experts at the University of Inappropriate Comparisons have conducted extensive research into some of the most popular toddlers' TV programmes, and have concluded that the lovable, pink, puny-legged porcine and her wonky-eyed family produce an effect on the brain more powerful than the white powder used by knobheads, celebrities, and celebrity knobheads.

What's more, they shockingly conclude that watching *In the Night Garden* gives an effect similar to LSD, and that watching just five minutes of *Dora the Explorer* causes pain similar to being kicked four times consecutively in the testicles by the hind legs of a mountain goat.

Researcher Helen Earth explained that their research centred on a network of hidden cameras installed in twenty-two homes across Berkshire. Helen explained, 'We were originally planning to just focus our research on two volunteer homes, but when ordering the hidden cameras, someone, who shall remain nameless, accidentally ordered twenty-two instead of two. When they arrived, we felt it best to expand our research accordingly – and we were glad we did, because we found some incredible, scientifically significant results.'

The week before some popular kids' TV channels were installed into the test houses, researchers found that the subject parents were constantly needing to entertain their toddlers, primarily by pushing colourful plastic things around the living room, and reading / prodding books with titles such as *That's Not My Dog / Cat / Monkey / Donkey / Bear / Car / Spaceship / Vodka / Boiler / Bluetooth Headset / Radiator / Locking Wheel Nut.* Some parents were seen feeding their children with home-cooked meals, taking trips to the park, pushing them around in cars, and teaching them words and phrases.

On Day One of the experiment, a range of popular kids' TV channels were installed into each house, and all other channels scrambled between the hours of 7 a.m. and 7 p.m. Within hours, researchers noticed some significant changes in the behaviour of the toddlers subjected to Nick Jr Too. Assistant Researcher Mini Mumwage described some of the footage she had ploughed through: 'As soon as *Peppa Pig* came on, the toddlers stopped playing with their toys and sat motionless on the sofa until the episode ended, as if transfixed by the pink piggy protagonists. As soon as the credits ended, the toddlers would leave the sofa and start playing with their toys again. It was quite freaky to watch.'

During these five minute segments of peace, parents started to find that they could do things that would otherwise not have been possible. One parent could be seen doing some washing-up. Another parent ate a chocolate biscuit in full view of their child. One parent even managed to take a piss without their toddler pointing and saying 'willy'.

Day Two of the test gave the first indication that something was happening within the toddlers' brains, as most of them could be heard waking up in the morning and shouting 'piiiiiiiiiiiiiiiiig' repeatedly until the TV was turned on, and then reacting in quite a distressed manner when all that could be found was the curiously punctuated *Alvin!!!!!!!!!!!! And the Chipmunks.* Mini revealed, 'It became clear that, whereas on Day One the toddlers wanted to watch *Peppa Pig*, by Day Three, the toddlers *needed* to watch *Peppa Pig*. And not just one double-episode, but three or four episodes back-to-back.'

It wasn't just the toddlers who were being impacted, either. Footage from Day Four showed one parent ignoring the door-bell because she was intent on finding out if George Pig's missing dinosaur would be found (it was, fortunately, up a tree). Meal times were becoming more ad-hoc, with home-cooked meals being replaced with oat bars and bananas fitted into the tiny window of time between episodes, during the Vanish Tip Exchange and Lelli Kelly adverts. Trips to the park turned into a few minutes in the garden, squeezed in when *Lily's Driftwood Bay* or *When Henry Met...* was on. *That's Not My Duckbilled Platypus* was replaced with *Peppa's Birthday Party*, and games involving plastic toys were replaced with temper tantrums involving the throwing of plastic toys when *Peppa Pig* episodes ended.

A number of parents, even after their toddlers had gone to bed, could still be seen watching *Peppa Pig*. One football-obsessed father even missed three minutes of Euro 2016 pre-match build-up by Glen Hoddle and Emmanuel Petit, as he was so intent on finding out whether a mate could be successfully found for Goldie, Peppa's Goldfish. He was tragically left with a very minimal grasp of Glen's vital views on Wayne Rooney's role in the 'diamond formation', and was almost clueless on Emmanuel's expert opinion on the use of a 'False Nine'. A mum could be seen attempting to buy the fictional computer game *Happy Mrs. Chicken* on Amazon during an exciting part of *Quantico*.

On Day Seven, Nick Jr Too was switched off for good, and toddlers and parents were left to go 'cold turkey'. There were cold sweats, tears, incomprehensible screaming and bizarre mood swings. The toddlers also struggled.

One parent took extreme measures and downloaded an illegal copy of Ben & Holly's Little Kingdom to take the edge off his cravings. Another parent took their toddler to a local petting zoo, and could be seen hugging and attempting to converse with a real-life pig, albeit with limited success. One family even went to Peppa Pig World and spent over one-hundred pounds to queue in excess of an hour for each of the four rides that they had time to go on.

All test families are now being weaned from their addictions by trained counsellors, who are using the slightly less addictive *Paw Patrol* to help reintegrate them back into society.

Those families who were left to view nothing but episodes of *In the Night Garden* had a more confusing time. Although the effect on the toddlers was similar – glazed eyes, drooling mouths, temporary deafness – parents could be seen staring at their offspring with an embarrassed disbelief. One mother could be heard muttering, 'I grew you for nine pissing months, went through three days of labour, and have spent the last eighteen months teaching you about the world and THIS is the kind of shit that you enjoy watching?!'

Mini explained that '*In the Night Garden* is such unmitigated bollocks, that the only possible explanation for toddlers being transfixed by it is that CBeebies must be transmitting some form of hidden, mind-controlling messages within the broadcast, much like in the later Beatles albums.'

Finally, those families subjected to the nauseatingly perky *Dora the (Pissing) Explorer* lasted just one day of the experiment, as regrettably all of the subject parents had gouged out their own eyes by lunchtime. But each one reported that they could still feel Dora's cold, dead eyes staring at them at all times, and researchers say that this is something that is likely to haunt them for the rest of their lives.

'The way that Dora constantly stares at the viewer with her massive, brown, psychotic deer eyes is genuinely disturbing. Couple that with three of the main characters being a monkey, a map and a backpack, the seemingly random use of Spanish words, and a constant attempt at trying to interact with the completely disinterested viewer, and it's a recipe for disaster. People just don't need that shit in their lives,' revealed Helen.

All families are now recovering well from their ordeals.

AUTHOR BIO:

James Hopes lives in the UK and is dad to a lively, and slightly cheeky, pre-schooler. In the gaps between work and trying to convince his little one to eat his dinner and stop climbing on things, his passions include music, football and writing. James is a regular writer at the *Huffington Post*, along with some local women's football websites. He blogs at *www.alifejustordinary.com* and co-runs *www.youhavetolaugh.com*, both of which focus on the funny side of parenting.

School Run Section Added To Driving Theory Test

Police and Road Safety Campaigners today welcomed the news from the Department of Transport that, as of December 1st this year, all drivers will be required to pass the new School Run section of the Theory Test. This news comes as commuters and parents get ready for the hell that is Back to School.

A spokesperson for the department said, 'After consultation with insurers, the police and school boards, we feel the new section added to the Theory Test will make the roads safer at school run times, both for drivers and pedestrians.'

At this time, exact details of the questions that will be asked were unavailable, but we were able to gain an insight into the sort of questions that will be included.

For example:

What should you do if Little Johnny announces he forgot his lunch box when you are two minutes away from the school gates?

A) Make a U turn and return home for the lunchbox.

B) Curse and tell him you will drop it into reception at break time.

C) Perform an emergency stop outside the Spar, turn on your hazard warning lights, and run in to buy a roll and drink, hoping the lights don't change before you are finished!

What should you do if Little Rose informs you she has homework due that hasn't been done yet?

A) Curse and tell her to do it now.

B) Get a notebook and pen and write a note to the teacher, whilst crawling in traffic, stating there was a family emergency and therefore no time for homework.

C) Ask her what the questions are and call out the answers.

School finishes at 3 p.m. What time do you arrive to collect your child?

A) 2:30 p.m.: I have to park at the front of the queue, even though my child will be last out.

B) 3 p.m.: I just sit in traffic until my child comes out.

C) Damnit, I knew there was something I had to do.

A letter has been sent home reminding parents not to park on double yellow lines outside the school gates. Do you:

A) Make a paper aeroplane out of it.

B) Use it to light the fire.

C) I pay my taxes, I'll park where I want.

In line with the new section of the Theory Test, there are also a number of new penalty point offences being introduced.

Some of the new penalty point offences are:

- Driver getting out of their car to walk their children to the pavement.
- Using a Range Rover or Jeep for the school run, if you are not a farmer.
- Talking to other parents out of car windows whilst in traffic.
- Ignoring horn-beeping of other motorists whilst doing any of the above.
- Using a hands-free kit that is so loud it causes waiting

parents to check their phones aren't ringing.

- Using indicators to let other drivers know what you are doing.
- Insisting the child puts a coat on. They are only going to use it as a goal post anyway.

A spokesman for the Police defended the new offences, saying this is not a money-making exercise. Research has shown that these offences lead to delays and road rage, costing the economy millions in insurance pay-outs and employee lateness.

Next week, we will be talking to commuters and parents about these changes and how it will affect them.

In other news, a German discount store has announced it will be launching a full school uniform for twenty pence!

AUTHOR BIO:
Alan LaCasse is a forty-two-year-old stepfather to two boys, and father to one boy and one girl. He blogs at *Omgitsagirl,* trying to make sense of raising a girl in a house of boys.

We Need to Talk About the Conditions of My Imprisonment

To the Secretary of State with Responsibility for Prisons,

I am three years into an eighteen year sentence. I have been told eighteen years is an approximation, and that it could be a lot longer than this: double, or even triple, depending on the state of the country when my eighteen years is up. I have been told that if there is no money/jobs/the housing market continues to skyrocket, these variables are likely to make my sentence longer. I must say that living with this uncertainty is the first thing I am writing to complain about, but I will deal with that later. I really need to talk about the conditions of my imprisonment.

It was agreed that, as a low risk offender (my crime was to have unrealistic romanticisms about what it is like to be a stay-at-home mum; I was also found in possession of generic baby sleep manuals, a crime against humanity), I would be able to complete my sentence under house arrest, with occasional day release for good behaviour. I was told I would be guarded night and day by two guards (they generally do not bother with night time, though, as they tend to get drunk on milk and pass out, only waking to make ridiculous demands, usually before passing out again). It is the behaviour of these two guards that I find intolerable, and a total breach of my human rights. Let me take you through a typical day…

The guards wake at a ridiculously early time, and often physically torture me into waking up. They will pull my hair, scratch my face, and rub snot and other bodily fluids all over me. Then they will laugh at themselves. I find this an abrupt way to be woken. Surely they could be informed that a simple call would do to wake me? They then proceed to torture me for the rest of the day, by going back to bed at various times themselves, but refusing to allow me to sleep. They put me to work straight away to their many tasks, which they scream at me to complete. This kind of sleep deprivation is the first of many tortures they inflict upon me.

They generally ask me to make at least three lots of breakfast for them - and never eat any of them - all whilst watching frightening and hypnotic things on the television, which I am sure, do nothing for their mental stability or professional development in their role as guards. They then spend a couple of hours trying to break into the snack cupboard (it is locked and they can't work out how to unlock it), and fighting each other. If I try to intervene, I will usually be physically assaulted again. I do not want them to know I have the key to the snack cupboard, as I feel smug knowing I have it, and that gives me a sense of power in a world where I am powerless.

They usually take me out for my day release mid-morning. We often go to church halls and other meeting places, to meet other prisoners in similar circumstances, all with their guards too. My guards do not tend to let me talk much to the other prisoners. I can only presume this is to inhibit any fun I may get from the outing, and to prevent any plotting of a bid for freedom. They also usually let me treat myself to a piece of cake but, just as I go to put it into my mouth, they will scream about how I dare to think I can eat cake in front of them, and demand it all for themselves. It is unnecessary to dangle a treat like that in front of a person, and then continually deny them the pleasure. But, Sir, they don't just stop there: should they find me in possession of any food, they will scream and scream until I give it to them. The same can be said for drinks.

At the end of some days, I have barely eaten, or taken any fluids, and this is in total breach of the terms of my imprisonment.

When we return from day release, having spoken very little to the other prisoners, and feeling stressed and hungry, the guards start getting drunk on milk again, and spend the next two hours taking it in turns to nap and sleep it off. I am usually exhausted by then, from the early wakeup and lack of food, but whichever guard happens to be up at any given time will demand that I entertain them, usually in the most energetic way possible. And is it really necessary that they accompany me *every* time I go to the toilet? There is no window in the toilet, I can't possibly escape, but there they are, every time I need a private moment of any sort, acting inappropriately (trying to flood the sink, unwrapping and eating tampons, etc.) because they know I can't get up to try and stop them. It is a disgrace.

For the rest of the afternoon, they appoint me Chief Entertainment Officer, which I have to say I did not know was outlined under the terms of my imprisonment agreement. I am running out of ideas, but I fear for my safety if I do not keep coming up with new and innovative entertainment. As if I was not exhausted enough.

We have the same routine at dinnertime: they demand various foods, before spitting them at me, dropping them on the floor and demanding I retrieve them... You must know the drill by now. They then spend the next couple of hours going absolutely batshit crazy. It is like they become possessed by the devil. I am worried for their mental health. I dread this time of day. Some of the other prisoners refer to it as the 'witching hour.'

Luckily, after the witching hour or two is over, they are totally and utterly knackered, and seem rendered incapable of inflicting any more physical or emotional torture upon me. They usually demand that I clean them, then they get drunk on their milk, and generally leave me alone for a couple of hours. I must say, Sir, that this is the only time I get to eat or drink, and do any of the recreational activities that I hear are provided to most people in the actual prisons. I also keep our surroundings clean and presentable, and basically do every household chore whilst in this captivity. I do the work of approximately one-hundred employees. I have heard that, in the large prisons, the prisoners get paid for the work they do around the prison. In three years, I have received nothing. What do you have to say to that?

I have a roommate, but he stumbles out of the door shortly after the torture-to-wake routine every morning, mumbling about tiredness and overwork. I can only assume he goes to some kind of work outside. When he gets back at the end of the day (he always misses the witching hour, and the cleaning and putting to bed of the guards), he still just mutters incoherently about his day, and then usually falls asleep shortly afterwards. Sometimes he is my only form of adult company, but he is usually snoring by the time the guards give us any time to speak to each other. I wish my roommate was not so tired all of the time, but that is the toll that his work, and the strict regime of the guards, is having upon him.

To conclude, Sir, I was wondering if a transfer to one of the actual prisons would be possible? I am not sure I can sustain this level of mental and physical torture, starvation, and lack of privacy. I am starting to fear for my own mental health, as it appears I have Stockholm Syndrome: I love and identify with the needs of my guards, despite what they inflict upon me. Is this normal? I feel that moving to another facility, even if just for a holiday, would be appropriate on this occasion, having regard to the massive breaches of human rights outlined above.

Yours sincerely,
A Stay-at-Home Inmate/Mother

AUTHOR BIO:

Lucy Wigley is a daydreaming, over-thinking wife to somebody who is constantly told he looks like Keifer Sutherland, and mum to a five-year-old Deep Thinker, and a four-year old Ninja In Training. During sleep deprived days, pacing the streets with a buggy containing her sleep-evading children, she started making up funny stories in her head. Someone suggested she write them down, and they turned into the award nominated blog *This Mum's Life*, which has also spawned an award nominated short film. Apart from her amazing husband and children, Lucy cites the near miss on the awards, and meeting Jeffrey Dean Morgan, as her best achievements to date.

The End

29446134R00057

Printed in Great Britain
by Amazon